CONSTRUCTING
A NEW NORMAL

Dealing Effectively with Losses
Throughout Life

Helen Reichert Lambin

Foreword by Carl Dehne, SJ

PUBLICATIONS

DEDICATED TO
Rev. Carl Dehne, SJ,
and Sr. Fran Glowinski, OSF,
in gratitude for their inspiration,
support, and friendship

CONSTRUCTING A NEW NORMAL
Dealing Effectively with Losses Throughout Life
Helen Reichert Lambin

Editing by Patricia A. Lynch and Gregory F. Augustine Pierce
Design and typesetting by Patricia A. Lynch

Scripture texts in this work are taken from *The Message: The Bible in Contemporary Language (Catholic/Ecumenical Edition)*, © 2013 by Eugene Peterson. Used with permission of NavPress.

Published by ACTA Publications, 4848 N. Clark St., Chicago, IL 60640, (800) 397-2282, www.actapublications.com

Library of Congress Number: 2014960080
ISBN: 978-0-87946-536-0
Printed in The United States by Total Printing Systems
Year: 25 24 23 22 21 20 19 18 17 16 15
Printing: 10 9 8 7 6 5 4 3 2 First

✪ Text printed on 30% post-consumer recycled paper

CONTENTS

FOREWORD

We know that all human beings, in the course of our lives, have to deal with days and seasons that are incredibly painful. These painful realities can be appropriately listed under the heading "loss." We lose loved ones in death—our parents, perhaps spouses and partners, siblings and friends, and—worst of all—sometimes even our own children. We outlive our animal companions. Deep and important relationships end— marriage, dear friendships, business and professional relationships. We change in relation to others, who are simultaneously changing in relation to us. We know failure and are forced to forego many of our hopes. Our careers can falter and die. We lose our looks, and our powers diminish. We can lose our health.

In all these painful passages, nothing is more comforting and healing to us than knowing a human being who has herself faced and successfully dealt with the painful losses that go with human life. Such a person may be full of useful hints and sparkling anecdotes, but what really counts is the available presence of someone who from her own experience knows what we are going through and simply by her healthy existence leads us to realize that we too can confront the worst and survive. And—more than that—prosper. Helen Lambin is such a dependable companion on the way, and we get to know her through her words in this book.

At the beginning, our favorite way of dealing with the losses that life entails is to pretend that after a time everything will be just the same as it was before—back to normal, as good as new. But as we live we learn, slowly and painfully, that our losses remain lost. We do not forget about them, we do not get over them, we cannot simply move on.

Helen Lambin teaches us that the way to deal with the pain of our losses is not some form of resignation. Rather, our task is to construct a new normal—new and in her case wonderfully unpredictable. Her nostalgia is not for a rich past in which she was wise enough to prevail over pain, but for a future she is busy creating. Her metaphor is pilgrimage, and her life story is an account of the journey of a convinced Christian seeking to live her faith in an honest and active way along unexpected paths. We have every reason to thank her for her witness in this book, and to thank the Lord for giving her to us.

Carl Dehne, SJ
Jesuit Community at Saint Louis University

1 SOONER OR LATER
Facing Losses Throughout Life

It is worth remembering that the time of greatest gain
in terms of wisdom and inner strength is often
the time of greatest difficulty.

— Dalai Lama

The words above are ones to wear like a favorite sweater or shawl. The insights of the Dalai Lama have illuminated universal truths and inspired people of many faiths, including Christianity, my own faith tradition. His words in this quote do not diminish or dismiss the effect of loss and painful transition in our lives. Loss is loss. Sorrow is sorrow. Pain is pain. But in helping us look at loss in a new way, he imbues our experience with a different meaning and a sense of hope.

You may be familiar with this popular saying: "If we all threw our problems in a pile and saw everyone else's, we'd grab ours back." I agree and disagree. Not all problems are created equal. I can't imagine applying this theory to a starving refugee driven from home by war and fearing still more violence. And I question applying it to someone like physicist Stephen Hawking, whose brilliant mind is trapped in a body devastated by Amyotrophic Lateral Sclerosis. At the same time, these words help us to see that, whatever our perspective, problems—including loss and transition—are part of life.

Sooner or later, if we live long enough, we are going to face some form of loss and transition. In fact, the longer we live, the more likely we will encounter these realities—major, minor, and in-between. Even young people are not immune. Even the much-too-young have faced loss and transition with resourcefulness and courage. And some of us may believe that older people can't cope with change. I disagree. Of course, they (I should saw *we*) can cope, having experienced change over our entire lifetime.

The question for people of all ages is: *How* do we cope?

Most of the chapters in this book are about loss and more-or-less painful transition. (It's almost impossible to separate the two). Some chapters are about other things—incarnation, islands, love, and tattoos. And yes, some are about hope. Most of the losses and transitions I describe are from my own experiences and from those of close friends and family members.

Over the years, I have written about various subjects, including travel (occasionally) and baseball (once). When people have asked me what I write about, I usually respond, after some thought, that I write primarily about loss and transition. But on reflection, I have come to realize I am writing resurrection theology. I don't know if a theologian would call it that, but I do. Resurrection underlies the way I write about loss and transition and, perhaps still more fundamentally, the way I have survived the challenges in my own life. This is what I hope to share.

Again, the question for all of us is: *How* do we cope?

Sometimes we cry out: "Lord, how can you allow this to happen to them, to us, to me?" That's a natural response. A human response. Don't worry. God can take it, just as he or she did with the cries of the psalmists almost three millennia ago.

Before I began writing this book, I wrote a prayer or reflection, thinking it might be a good fit. It goes like this:

Lord Jesus Christ, Son of God. How could this have happened to you? This terrible suffering and this brutal, humiliating, lonely death. Abandoned by your most of your friends, at least for a time, that terrible time. Regarded by many as a failure. Some say you offered yourself as a sacrifice for us sinners, a sacrificial lamb, the Lamb of God. But you are the Son of God! You share not only God's divinity but our humanity. Wouldn't a drop or two of your blood have sufficed? Wouldn't the ordinary cares of daily living have been enough? Or, did you suffer so that when we come to you in pain and suffering, for ourselves or for others, that we know you fully understand? You suffered so that we cannot say to you: "But you don't understand. How *could* you? You are the Son of God." So that we *can* say, *must* say instead: "God who suffered, be with me, be with us at this time. And help me to be with and for others in their time."

And, oh yes, remember what came after Christ's suffering and death—Act II, so to speak. Unimaginable but wholly imaginative. Incredible and credible. So startling that we are still talking about it 2,000 years later. Hope. Joy. Wonder. Confusion. Surprise. What happened was totally unexpected. It was *much better* than expected. It was The Resurrection, with a capital "T."

Meanwhile, back to Act I.

2 LOSS AND TRANSITION
Remembering and Response

Some problems are so complex that you have to be highly
intelligent and well-informed just to be undecided about them.
— Laurence J. Peter

"Get over it."

Spoken or unspoken, this is too often one reaction to our expression of lingering grief or pain—at least that which lingers longer than others *think* it should. This grief or pain could be related to the death of a loved one, the loss of a job, serious health problems, a broken relationship, the myriad sorrows that can come along in life. Regardless of the reason, grief doesn't follow a schedule.

I believe in a free society and generally don't believe in banning books, but there are two phrases I'd like to restrict, if not ban. The first is, "Get over it." If each of us were allowed to use these words only three times in a lifetime, we'd have to give some serious consideration to the time, place, and circumstances. (The other phrase I'd restrict is the dismissive, "I've moved beyond that in my thinking.")

Many of us do not do well with loss and painful transitions. We are, for the most part, optimistic people. That is a good outlook, but we expect every difficulty to have a silver lining—immediately. That, of course, is not the way life works. Dealing with suffering, rejection, pain, and loss are necessary steps in the transition to joy, healing, and acceptance. That was true for Jesus in his transition through suffering to the ultimate joy of Easter.

It's almost impossible to separate loss and transition. All profound loss involves some kind of transition, but not all transition involves profound loss.

Generally speaking, I like the word *transition*. Life is not static, but dynamic. That is, it involves change and growth. What would life be without the possibility of change?

Some transitions are positive: we work for them, plan for them, and look forward to them. Think, for example, of graduation, marriage, voluntary retirement, moving to a place of our choosing, a first apartment, the birth of a child, a new relationship, freedom from a painful relationship, a long-awaited vacation or journey, a new pet, or the simple pleasure of awakening to a new day.

But planning, anticipation, and hopeful waiting do *not* apply to painful transitions—the loss of a job, the relocation of a friend or relative, the breaking-up of a cherished relationship. And it certainly does *not* apply to the death of a loved one.

Our difficulty in dealing with loss and transition—or helping others to do so—has consequences for individuals and society as a whole. As members of a society, we can find our compassion and will to help others diminished. As individuals, we can become cynical, burned out, depressed, or resigned.

We are all going to face some kind of loss sooner or later. Some of us will face more than others, surely, but no one is immune. Rather than allowing or encouraging ourselves—or others—to become paralyzed by loss or painful transition, we need to find a way to move through it and beyond. We may want simply to get back to normal, but we can't go back. We have to construct to a *new* normal, a normal that often is built brick by brick.

Scripture teaches us that for all things there is a season. And yes, that includes a season to mourn. And yes, our faith tells us that even in darkness God is with us.

Think of God's words at the beginning of Isaiah 43. God does not say: "Get over it." Instead, God tells us: "Don't be afraid, I've redeemed you. I've called you by name. You're mine. When you're in over your head, I'll be there with you. When you're in rough waters, you will not go down." Or take to heart Jesus' words in Matthew 11:28: "Come to me. Get away with me and you'll recover your life. I'll show you how to take a real rest."

When I say that I am writing from a faith perspective, I don't mean that I am going to speak of God constantly. I'm not. It's not that I have never had doubts—I do—but, for me, faith is like the oxygen. Without it I'd find myself gasping for breath as if I were at a very high altitude, like Pike's peak.

A disclaimer. I have written about loss, transition, and prayer for some twenty years. I am not a psychologist or theologian, but I hope the experiences and insights I share in this book will help you move through loss and painful transition or offer support to someone who is sad or lost. After all, like it or not, we're all in this together.

I have experienced profound joy and profound loss for over seven decades. Transitions expected and unexpected, welcome and most unwelcome. I am or have been wife, widow, mother, grandmother, writer, mistake-maker, and adult learner. As I discover daily, I still have a lot to learn. In another society at this age I could be considered a crone and a wisdom figure. I probably can qualify as a crone but, as much as I would like to qualify as a wisdom figure, I know better.

I have moved beyond that in my thinking.

3 'TIS BETTER TO HAVE LOVED
Love and Loss In General

> I hold it true, whatever befall;
> I feel it, when I sorrow most;
> 'tis better to have loved and lost
> than never to have loved at all.
> — Alfred Lord Tennyson

These much loved lines are from Tennyson's poem, "In Memoriam," written after the death of his friend Arthur Hallam in 1833, a loss that left Tennyson profoundly depressed. Tennyson survived the loss and depression and kept on writing, publishing this poem seventeen years later in 1850, the year he was named poet laureate of England.

Tennyson got it right. Loss is painful, sometimes terrible, even agonizing. Surviving it can seem impossible; enduring it can seem endless. Few of us, however, would want to take a pass on loss, because it is also the price of love—of love given, of love received, of love remembered. Consider two points about loss.

First, loss has its price, but you don't have to pay endlessly. The only way *past* loss is *through* it. Think of what you go through when you cross any difficult or frightening obstacle—a swamp, a busy intersection, a rocky hill, or a slippery surface. You may need to summon up your courage, do some planning, and acquire a skill to maneuver it. The same with loss. Facing it and moving ahead is usually the only way to get to the other side—to continue with life with meaning. This doesn't mean you can't or shouldn't accept help—counseling or medication as warranted—but it *does* mean letting yourself experience grief without feeling guilty or inadequate about it. If grief becomes paralyzing or destructive, it can become a form of illness, but in most cases sorrow is not an illness but a part of life. Just as love is a part of life, so is loss. Just as joy is a part of life, so is sadness.

Even if you can't see the path ahead, rest assured that the path is there. We, like Tennyson, *can* survive loss and continue to do some—perhaps even many—of the things we hold dear. We might even discover new sources of meaning in our everyday lives. We do this both *in spite* of and *because* of our experience of love and loss, of survival and compassion. We can't all be poet laureates of England, but we can bring our own gifts to our own place and time. Call it being poet laureates of our own lives.

Second, I also hold strongly that loss does not kill love. It only changes the way we experience love. Of course, it limits our experience. No letters, no phone calls, no shared meals, no emails, no text messages, no hugs. We can't see or hear our loved ones—generally speaking—but they are there.

At age eighty (good grief, can that be true?), I have had my share of losses. I lost my father when I was twenty-five, my mother some thirty years later, and, five years after that, my husband. I have also lost cherished relatives, friends, and several pets.

I have recently become interested in cosmology—great big things like galaxy clusters and itty-bitty things like quarks. I understand only a fraction of what I read, but I can live with my ignorance. My ignorance can restrict, but it can also serve as a foundation for learning something.

One of the really super big things we've learned from science over the centuries is that just because we can't see something doesn't mean it isn't there. When I was growing up in a small town in Iowa, the sky looked as if a giant hand had scattered stars across a black velvet sky. Season by season, constellations moved across the horizon—the Big and Little Dippers (or Great and Little Bear); Orion, the Hunter; Cassiopeia, the Lady in the Chair; and those Seven Dancing Sisters, to name a few—the same stars and clusters that were seen when our remote ancestors sat around a fire or when the shepherds in Luke's infancy narratives heard angels singing as they watched their flocks.

In all the years I have lived in a city, the city lights have prevented me from seeing the heavenly lights. Once in a while I get a glimpse. I have seen Jupiter, shining proud because of its size and proximity to earth. And I might have seen a bit of Orion's belt. But the others? They're still there—beyond my vision, but still there. And if this is true of what we have been able to see, what about what we've never seen but is known to us through science? Galaxies far beyond our range of vision that are visible by only the most sophisticated of telescopes. Dark matter that exerts gravity but can't be seen even by those powerful telescopes. And what about all those sub-atomic particles, what my daughter Rosemary calls "stuff that isn't stuff"?

In short, I have no trouble believing in the unseen, the invisible. The Scottish writer John Buchan once described an atheist as one who "has no invisible means of support." As a person of faith, I thank God for being my invisible means of support. I wouldn't have weathered life's losses and transitions without it.

When my husband, Henry, died, a Jesuit friend sent me a card with a comforting metaphor. As a ship sails away and approaches the horizon, it disappears from our sight. As far as we can see, it's no longer there, but on the other side of the horizon, people see the sails and cry out, "Here they come!"

This is my hope and my belief—for you, for me, for all who have loved and lost: At some time, out of time, those we have loved but haven't lost forever will be looking, waiting, and watching, until they shout with joy: "Here they come!"

4 LAMENTATION IN RAMAH
Loss of a Child

A sound was heard in Ramah, weeping and much lament, Rachel weeping for her children, Rachel refusing all solace, Her children are gone, dead and buried.

— Matthew 2:18

These words from Matthew's infancy narrative refer to the Massacre of the Innocents—King Herod's calculated killing of Jewish males under the age of two following the birth of Jesus. Scripture scholars can debate the historical basis of the story, but no one can debate the pain of grieving parents, pain that echoes down the centuries.

I have had personal experiences with most of the losses and transitions in this book, but I have not been through the loss of a child, a profoundly painful kind of loss. I have had a glimpse—and I emphasize *glimpse*—of what it might feel like to lose a child, but I could never say and should never say, "I *know* how you feel." I can only *imagine*. The closest I have come to this happened more than forty years ago when I lost hold of my of three-year-old son Joe's hand in the New York subway at morning rush hour. One minute he was there. The next minute he was not. The platform was filled with people. The trains roared by. I called his name in increasing desperation. Four decades later, I can still remember how those minutes—or seconds—felt. A lot of people must have heard me calling, but one person—make that *angel*—answered. Out of the crowd came a tall African-American man, leading my little blonde boy by the hand. This particular angel was wearing a business suit—no wings—but to me and my family, he will always be God's messenger.

For months after this frightening experience, I would wake up in the middle of the night, afraid one of the children was missing. After more than forty years, I can still remember my terror, and the feeling of total disbelief. *This cannot be happening, this cannot be happening. Not to my child. Not to any child.*

We feel we should be able to protect our children—whatever their age—from pain, illness, accidents, and death. Children stop being children, but parents never stop being parents. We expect, however unwillingly, that sooner or later we will lose some of those we love and that we too will join them, but we do not expect to outlive our children. They are out past and our present. We expect they will be a part of our future. When a child dies, there are no easy answers, especially if the child is *your* child.

Even parents who were extraordinarily close to God were not exempt from loss. John, long awaited son of Elizabeth and Zachary, was sent to prison and beheaded. Mary, wife of Joseph and mother of Jesus, lived to see her son executed in the most brutal, terrifying, degrading death imaginable: death by crucifixion. All seemed lost—her son, all hope. Her grief was unimaginably painful, but it was not, as it turned out, permanent. There was an unimaginable outcome: She lived to see him live again. In the resurrection, death had been conquered for all and for all time.

We can be reluctant to mention the child's name to a grieving parent for fear it will be a reminder of the loss, but a parent doesn't *need* a reminder. The memory will always be there. We should be attentive to spoken and unspoken cues, allowing parents to share in their own way and in their own time. One day, someday, the distance between them and their child will be bridged. In the meantime, they draw consolation and strength from God's promises: "Look! Look! God has moved into the neighborhood, making his home with men and women! They're his people, he's their God. He'll wipe every tear from their eyes. Death is gone for good—tears gone, crying gone, pain gone—all the first order of things gone" (Revelation 21:3-4).

Many years ago, when I was not long out of high school, a friend of mine died of leukemia. His name was Hughie. He was only about eighteen, a truly nice, bright kid. We had dated and were friends. I knew his father, who worked at high school basketball games, but when Hughie died, I couldn't bring myself to speak to the dad. I evaded and delayed, ducking into a store or an alley when I saw him. I just didn't know what to say. How could this have happened? What if I made him feel worse? Eventually my mother convinced me that I couldn't and shouldn't put it off any longer. The next time I saw Hughie's dad, I summoned up my courage and crossed the street to speak to him. I told him what a truly nice, bright guy his son had been. *He was.* I told him how much Hughie's friendship meant. *It did.* And how sorry I was. Then his father took my hand and thanked me, telling me how glad he was I had spoken of his son. This was a lesson I have never forgotten.

Time is one of the common threads running through loss and healing. Grieving takes time. Healing takes time. We need time, little by little, to accept the small joys that come into our lives. Healing also takes support and recognition of the past—the child *lived*—and the present—the child *now lives* in a different way. And that *different way* makes an immense difference to survivors.

In recent years we have witnessed one mass murder after another, many involving children and a heavily-armed gunman. I live in a city where children die violent deaths almost every week, sometimes every day. I see the grief-ravaged faces of their family members on the local news. No child should have to live in fear of dying by violence or even from hunger or preventable disease. No parent should have to live in fear of losing a child in any of these ways.

As a result of my decision to get some tattoos later in life (more on this later!), I often find myself in conversation with interesting young people—nice young people of different ethnicities, races, and backgrounds who have questions or comments (polite ones, I should add). When I hear of a child being killed, I often think, "What if this is one of the kids I've met on the street, on the el, on the bus?"

How can we break the cycle of violence and untimely death? More equitable distribution of wealth and resources? More accessible and affordable mental health resources? Education? Gun control? Conflict resolution? These complex issues challenge even the experts. I am not an expert, but I think we have to ask ourselves this question: "What if this were *my* child?" Do we join in a candlelight vigil, leave flowers at the scene of the crime, attend the funeral or memorial service, or offer comforting words to the grieving family? Yes. These are signs and symbols of compassion, and we should perform them when we can.

But the big question is: Do we stop there or do we take action?

We all have to work together so that in Ramah, or in Chicago, in any city or village, Rachel will no longer heard weeping for her children.

5 HOW DO I LOVE THEE?
Death of a Spouse or Life Companion

How do I love thee?
Let me count the ways.
— **Elizabeth Barrett Browning**

Above are the first two lines of Sonnet Number 43, one of the most famous poems by Elizabeth Barrett Browning. She and her husband, the noted English poet Robert Browning, contributed immensely to English literature—and to each other's lives.

"How do I miss thee? I can't begin to count the ways." These are the words of almost anyone who has lost a beloved spouse or life companion.

Love is wonderful. It really does help make the world go round. It sets heart and hope and happiness in motion. But it can also lead to an achy, shaky heart. I am not trying to sound like a country western singer—although I do like some country western music—but I think "achy, shaky" is an accurate description of the potent feeling of one of the first stages after the loss of a husband or a wife.

Such small things can set it off—that achy, shaky feeling that makes your heart lurch and takes your breath away. Such small things and so many years later. The smell of autumn, Christmas lights in a neighbor's window, the sound of piano music he or she liked or played, family photos. We each have our own small things and or our own ways of dealing with them.

My husband, Henry, has been dead more than nineteen years as I write this chapter—nineteen years. He died suddenly on January 20, 1996. (Even today that date is a very mixed bag—the day of his death and the day of our youngest daughter's birthday.) But I remember. I remember that achy, shaky feeling. So do many others who have experienced this kind of loss.

I thought I might have to work at bringing back some of those early feelings from the first years after Henry's death in order to write properly and honestly about it. I didn't even have to try. The feelings and memories come unbidden, though not all the time. And I still miss him. A world with Henry in it was surely better than one without, but I am thankful for every happy day, every ordinary day I have. Like yesterday. And today. And hopefully many tomorrows. I know Henry would want it that way. But still, the reminders of him come—unbidden and when least expected.

Not long after Henry's death, a friend asked, "Does it bother you when people bring up their own losses at this time?" "No," I answered. "I think it is inevitable." That was one time when I got it completely right. However sympathetic—or empathetic—we may be, other peoples' losses remind us of our own. I didn't mind this thoughtful question, but I did and continue to mind a much less sensitive, much less thoughtful question: "Are you over it now?" Well-intended or otherwise, this is not a good question. I didn't say it at the time, but this is what I felt like saying: "No, I'm not over it now. It was death, not a bad cold. And I don't think I'll actually be over it unless I see Henry walk up the back steps once again, wearing his raincoat and Greek fisherman's hat, carrying his tattered briefcase." No, I didn't say it. But I wanted to.

When Henry died, I was a couple of months short of sixty-two. Given the longevity of some of the women and men in my extended family, I figured I might live for another thirty years or even more without him. The thought was absolutely overwhelming. To face this reality, I did was what I often do when faced with what appears to be a big job: I broke it into smaller parts, first dividing the 30 years into months, 360 of them, on an imaginary grid, 12 across, 30 down. Then I began counting: *One month down, two months (1/180th of my expected life span) and I'm still standing.... Six months down (or 1/60th)....* And so on. In time I was counting less often, but still counting until, after two years, I no longer needed to count. It worked for me for the short term, but it clearly, was not—is not—a long-term solution. It had gradually dawned on me that simply marking off time was no way to live life, no way to live the gift of time. I changed my focus to doing what I wanted to do and being who I wanted to be. Now. Without him. Temporarily.

Nineteen of those theoretical thirty years have now passed, and I am glad to be alive and grateful for the gift of the days and years I've had—the times of joy, sorrow, anxiety, anger, contentment, confusion, in other words, the gift of everyday life. I know that Henry would have wanted me to live well, and I am ever grateful to him for all his love, which still sustains me every day.

Do I still miss him? Of course. How could I not? I still think of things I'd like to tell him, things I'd like to ask him. Sometimes, for a very brief moment, I'm back in time—or maybe in another time—and I think,"I'll have to tell Henry that. He'll be interested...." And then I remember I'm in *this* time. After I catch my breath, I do the one thing I still can do: I tell him anyway.

One of the most difficult facets of the loss of a spouse or life partner is precisely this: the loss of love and support, the special relationship of your Number One Person (for example, my husband) to his Number One Person (for example, me). Without Henry, I've had to find new ways to enjoy life once again. As I said, I have had to discover how I can be complete in myself, as a human person. I have and will continue to do so.

I opened this chapter with a quote, and I'm going to conclude with a couple of quotes, pearls of wisdom given to me in the early days of my grief.

One is from the leader of a support group for those experiencing loss. "You don't get over it. You learn to live with it." It's a good summary of the grieving process. And if sounds bleak, it isn't. You *can* learn to live with it, and live well, with joy and sorrow, contentment and boredom, a sense of normalcy. But first you have to redefine *normal,* and redefining *normal*—that takes time.

Another pearl is from a widowed friend, Dorothy W. Shortly after Henry's death, she said, "I know you won't believe this now, but it does get better. It won't always be this bad." Dorothy has passed on herself, but she was and continues to be right. Even though someone in the early stages of grief may find it as hard to believe as I did, it *does* get better—as long you are to *willing* to let it get better. Like a waltz—a couple of steps forward, then a step or two back—it doesn't happen all at once or in a predictable way. At first, it can be hard to even think of doing anything you could enjoy. And then, when you *do* something—especially something you *would have* liked doing in the past. The feeling is something like this: "I *could have* enjoyed it, if only _____ (fill in the name) could have been there with me or waiting for me at home." And then suddenly, one day, one hour, when you least expect it, you discover something amazing. "Here and now, at this moment, I am content." These are times to welcome and rejoice. Yes, there will be other times for grieving. "There's an opportune time to do things, a right time for everything under heaven" (Ecclesiastes 3:1). But appreciate the good moments and hope for a season of more of them.

My final quote in this section is from the last lines of the poem that opened this chapter.

I love thee with the breath,
Smiles, tears, of all my life!—and, if God choose,
I shall but love thee better after death.

I am not suggesting—most emphatically *not* suggesting—that we do anything by any means to hurry along our reunion with our loved one. Our lives are in God's hands. Remember Ecclesiastes? Sometimes, it seems to me, the author can be really grouchy, but sometimes he really has it right. As Ecclesiastes says, "There's an opportune time to do things, a right time for everything under heaven: A right time for birth and another for death.... A time to cry and another to laugh, A time to lament, and a time to cheer..." (Ecclesiastes 3:1-2, 4).

What I am suggesting—most emphatically *am* suggesting—is that death does not kill love: not in the person who has passed on, and not, as we who have mourned well know from experience, in the hearts of those of us who survive them. What I am suggesting is that someday, in due season, in *God's* season, there will be a time to "cheer"—or at least be more quietly happy. Scripture, tradition, and a host of theologians remind us that in Jesus' resurrection we are all called to a new life—a new life that begins here and now, a new life to be lived for ourselves and for others. (The *shared* vision is part of the deal.)

In my book *Death of a Husband*, I included a story called "The Unset Clock and the Wound-Up Dog." I'll try to summarize it here.

A widow, alone in the house three weeks after her husband's death, paces the floor on a Saturday evening, wondering how she will ever get through this. She takes a hot bath and turns back her bed, lamenting (yet again) to her spouse. "If only you were here. How am I going to live without you?" There is no answer. "If only I knew that you were all right...that you are as happy as you deserve to be." But once again there is no answer. She sees a tail disappear around the corner and remembers that she forgot to take the dog out. And she remembers that once upon a time her husband would have set the alarm for 10:15 so that he would wake up to walk the dog.

And then, suddenly, inexplicably, the alarm clock begins to ring in an empty room, the alarm that has been silent and unset for three weeks. And when she lets the dog out, the dog barks joyously to be let back in. This is remarkable! She and her husband had been trying to teach this very dog to bark at the back door so that she wouldn't wait in silence and cold if one of them forgot to let her back in.

The story concludes with some reactions to the event. Some people thought it was wonderful. Some said they could explain it rationally. But the widow just smiled, listening and remembering. Could her friends explain it? Maybe. But probably not. Because they weren't there when the alarm clock rang in the silence and the dog barked in joyous greeting on the empty stairs.

Readers often ask me if that story is true. They clearly hope it is. "Yes," I tell them, "it is true." "How do you know?" is the next question. "Because," I answer, "the widow in the story is me."

6 OUR LOST GENERATION
The Passing of Our Parents

Time goes, you say? Ah, no! Alas. Time stays, we go.
— Henry Austin Dobson

These words are from the poem *Paradox of Time*, the inspiration for *The Fountain of Time*, the majestic Laredo Taft sculpture in Chicago's Washington Park. The sculpture is composed of 100 figures, representing humanity from the dawn of woman and man up to the present (then the 1920s). I can't speak with certainty about time. Einstein said it is the fourth dimension. Some scientists say time is not linear but past, present, and future all wrapped up in the same moment. Don't ask me to explain it. But I do know that whatever time is up to, we keep on moving on. It is inevitable that the generation before us, including our parents, will eventually pass away. This is how it is and will be, but it doesn't mean we have to like it. We are never really old enough or ready enough to be orphans.

Sometimes the loss of a parent is sudden, sometimes a slow fading away, and sometimes an erosion of the personality by one or another form of dementia. Neither my parents nor grandparents suffered from dementia, although both sides of the family had and have their fair share of life-long eccentrics. Including me. Dementia, however, has afflicted others I have known and cherished: spouses and parents of friends, friends themselves.

However the loss of a parent happens, it's still a loss. While grieving for a mother or father is painful, it would be even more painful if you didn't or couldn't feel grief for what had been. We don't want our children to succumb to prolonged sadness at our passing, but we certainly want them to feel bad—at least sometimes and in some ways—at the loss of our physical presence. That is, we don't want our children to evade the pain of grief, but we don't want them to carry it too far either. We want our children to be able to deal with our death effectively and to mention us fondly now and then—and perhaps with a dose of humor.

When my father died, I was twenty-five, living several hundred miles away. I never really got to know Dad, adult to adult, but I remember his kindness, gentleness, interest in things like history and Native American life and railroads and pioneering. I wish I had spent more time with him. I wish my children would have gotten to know him, and he would have gotten to know them as well. And I wish my widowed mother could have had more decades as his wife.

My mother died when I was fifty-six. I am so grateful that I did get to know her as an adult. As a young child, I thought she was terrific. As a teen and young adult, I found her presence and rather commanding self annoying at times. (Amazing as it may seem, I suspect that I was probably equally annoying, being my usual resistant self.) But in later years, as a parent myself, I was able to enjoy her company and her presence not only as a daughter but also as a friend. We could laugh together, at each other, and at ourselves. We could discuss politics and religion, current events and food—especially comfort food she might make for me. I liked the order and peace of her home—an order I had not appreciated years earlier.

After she died and before her phone was disconnected, I would dial her phone number just to hear it ring, even though I knew it was ringing in an empty room, in an empty apartment.

I like being a reasonably independent person; I like having autonomy—a nice way of saying I don't like being told what to do. What I don't like is being the *older* generation. Even my aunts and uncles are gone. Not only do my nephews and one niece have children, but one grandnephew and his wife have a child, which makes me, I think, a great great aunt. I am very happy for them, but that is rather a lot of "greats" for me. Where can I turn when I want some *adult* wisdom from someone more grown up than I am?

I am beginning to think that my mother and father have been rather derelict in their duties. Don't get me wrong. I love my parents. I am grateful to them for their love and work and joys and sacrifices, but where are they now, at the times when I need them? Is the fact that my mother would be over one hundred and my father a decade older than her a reasonable excuse? I am kidding, of course. That is not the world as it is.

But it seems to me, at times, on some days, when the moon is right or the wind is light, that I should be able to go visit them once again. I should be able to pack a few clothes, go downtown to Union Station, and hop on a train to Iowa, watching the lights of towns and farms flicker by in the darkness, hearing the crossing signal whistle again and again—three longs, a short and a long—as the train takes me home. But the trains to Marion, Iowa, are long gone. Now I would have to drive instead, crossing the Mississippi at the beautiful wide-river crossing at Savannah and then travelling another hour to reach "home."

My mother would be there with my father. They would be as I remember them when I was younger—actually they might be even younger than I am now. And we would sit around the table to share a good dinner cooked by my mother, not me (after all, I am the baby of the family), catching up on all the family news. And I would be able to draw on some senior wisdom from someone more senior than me. Does that seem too much to ask once in a while?

On one of my last visits with Mom, she told me about a recurring dream. My father had worked in the railroad office, and in her dream he was walking along railroad tracks ahead of her. Usually she would call out his name, but he either couldn't hear her or wouldn't turn around. In the most recent dream, however, he had turned and was waiting for her to catch up.

When my mother died, I told people that she was finally reunited with my father.

"Do you really believe that?" someone asked.

"Well, if it isn't that way when my mother gets there," I replied, "it will be. She'll shake her finger in the face of God and get everything straightened out."

Now and then my mother nags me from the beyond. As needed. For example, she used to say to me, "You can be big enough to build bridges, Helen Irene." Periodically, I still hear her saying those very words (or some other verbal blast from the past). After all, it's still her job. Death shouldn't mean that parental responsibilities come to an end. I intend to nag my children and granddaughter, only occasionally and always judiciously, not necessarily because I won't be able to mind my own business but to remind them that I am still alive in a real way. Hear that, kids? Love you.

7 WHO ARE YOU?
Radical Change in Personality

Oh, Johnny, I hardly knew ye.
— Irish folk song

Death and broken relationships are not the only kinds of loss, of course. Personality change is another. It's difficult enough when a change is expected or freely chosen, but it's even more challenging and most unwelcome when it involves cognitive ability, mental health, or brain function. When those we love no longer appear to be who or what they once were, our relationship with them can be disrupted, altered, or even lost. We probably all know people who have gone through this kind of change or are experiencing it at the present time. If the dysfunction is severe enough, we may feel as if we can't reach them. They are there, and yet they are not there.

Changes in personality and mental status can be the result of brain damage, Alzheimer's disease, other forms of dementia, substance abuse, a traumatic experience, an accident, a side-effect of a medication, a brain aneurysm, heart problems that cause lack of oxygen to the brain, and more. Whatever the cause, the end results are change and most certainly loss, a loss that ripples outward to include family members, caregivers, and friends.

The husband of a long-time friend of mine suffered from Lewy Body Dementia (LBD) in later life. Joe was very bright, humorous, thoughtful, and original, and was able to bring these same traits to bear in coping in the early stages of his illness. He was aware that those with late-onset LBD very often do not outlive the illness. Joe went to support groups with his very capable and loving wife. As time passed and the illness progressed, he confused the present with the past and sometimes was just plain confused. It hurt to see this happen to a friend. I can only imagine what it must have been like for him and for his family. And yet, somewhere in there was the person we all once knew.

Radical personality changes and the loss of self are certainly painful for loved ones, but they also have to be painful for the person himself or herself, seeming like death on the installment plan or living in a kind of limbo. The questions for loved ones linger. "Where did you go? How do I reach you? What is the right thing to do and not to do? How do I cope?" Caregiver support groups can help. So can caring friends.

Now and then so-called jokes about forgetfulness are intended to be witty, perhaps. They aren't. There is nothing funny about losing who you are or losing a loved one to any form of dementia. If you are the one who is suffering or if you care for and love someone who is suffering, feel free to laugh at your own situation. Dark humor can accompany dark times. I've used it myself as a widow. But no one outside the circle of suffering has a right to make light of a situation. I know that you, my readers, have too much class to do it anyway, but you might help others follow your lead.

"Some things never change." *Sigh.* "People don't change." *Shake of head.* Both quotes are widely-accepted popular wisdom. Both are partially true, but both can be largely wrong.

While this book is primarily about loss and painful transitions, some painful transitions can have a very positive outcome. Take, for example, a former substance abuser. We'll call him X because that isn't his name. His life was dominated by his drug of choice and how to get high. Eventually, he decided enough was enough. He wanted to turn his life around, and he did—not overnight but in time.

What a beautiful phrase: "in time." Take the case of St. Paul. After St. Paul was knocked onto his (ahem) posterior on the road to Damascus and encountered Christ, he wanted to change and did. But it was about fourteen years before he actually set off on his famous missionary journeys and began writing those letters we now read in the Bible. After X spent years working on turning his life around, he's at the point now of helping others to do the same. His mission is just starting.

I am not suggesting we need to accept statements of change at face value. People change through behavior, not words. I am simply suggesting we remain open to the possibility that people can and do change. And if other people change, even we can change.

Even change for the better can sometimes be difficult for other people. People who have lost a significant amount of weight and have reached a healthy level sometimes find their spouses or partners are threatened. How many recovering alcoholics or trying-to-quit smokers have been asked, "Can't you have *just one?*" An ex-smoker myself, I kept asking myself that same question, "Can't I have *just one?*" It took me five tries and some fifteen years to learn that I couldn't. (Not having the substances themselves can feel like a loss, but that's a loss you *can* actually get over.)

Unlike loss that comes through death or distance or through a completely broken relationship, the loss of someone through radical change in personality can be a loss-in-process. We don't have established prayers or rituals to deal with that kind of loss, although maybe there should be—maybe a repeatable ritual, a ritual with remembrance of the past and hope for the future—however that future develops.

Remember the friend I spoke of earlier, the man who had LBD? At a dinner one night with other old friends, conversation swirled around him. Everyone was making an effort to include him. Clearly, things were not the way they once were. He was with us and not with us. And yet, and yet, there was a moment when his wife reached over and put her hand on his. When he looked at her, it was a look of pure love. And in that look you could see that not only did he surely know who he was, but also, for the moment, he knew what she meant, had always meant, and always would mean to him. He has passed on now, and, I hope, passed in some ways into a new self—or perhaps I should say, a renewed self.

In the long run isn't that our deepest hope for ourselves, for everyone we love?

8 WHO AM I?
Changes in Our Identity

I am I, Don Quixote, the Lord of La Mancha. My destiny
calls, and I go! And the wild winds of fortune shall carry me
onward...to whithersoever they blow....Onward to glory I go!
— *Man of La Mancha, the Musical*

Change for worse, change for better. Or change TBA. But change *will* happen and with it our sense of who we are. Our sense of identity is rooted in our relationship with our significant other (or hoped-for significant other), faith, family, work, interests, location, experience, perceived status, appearance, and health—to name a few. Change, loss, or transition in any of these areas can lead to an identity crisis whether the change comes by choice or chance. With whom and with what do we identify? The answers can make a big difference in how we survive the inevitable challenges.

In the United States, we often identify people by their job or profession. What we do is certainly a part of who we are, but only a part. One of my French teachers once shared this bit of Gallic wisdom and grace. On meeting people for the first time, don't ask, "What do you do?" This is considered boorish, a way of ranking people by socio-economic standards. Instead, the teacher said, you might ask a question like, "What is your passion?"

I have been secretary, social worker, program coordinator, wife, mother, grandmother, widow, writer, volunteer, and all-around goof-off. I liked some of the jobs and love my family. Writing is a part of my identity, but for many years a strong part of that identity was wife. I *liked* being Mrs. Henry Lambin. I liked checking the *married* box on forms, and I still dislike checking *widowed*. The first time I checked *widowed* was on a tax form. Then and for so many times after that, I felt utterly diminished. Once upon a time I *was* somebody—somebody else! Now who was I? A *poor widow* immediately comes to mind. The "Merry Widow" waltz might be a lovely dance tune, but the "merry widow" concept is downright silly in real life. I made a conscious decision early on to refuse to be diminished, lessened, less than *Somebody*—even if the Somebody I had been was in process of becoming *Somebody Somewhat New*.

I am sure I wasn't aware of all the identity shifts in my life—and probably still have some to come. But I was aware (very aware at the time, or shortly thereafter) of three shifts in the last two decades.

One was retirement, a shift I liked. I had liked my job very much at the beginning, but a number of factors, including office location, changed over time. Five years earlier than my own retirement, I was glad the latest retiree wasn't me. Four years later, I was looking forward to taking (somewhat) early retirement. (Actually, it wasn't all that early. I was almost sixty-five.) My office at the time was in a rather dreary basement, with glass blocks for windows, and no way to let in some fresh air. I still remember walking to the local garden center that first day after retirement and thinking, "So this is how the sky looks. So this is how the air smells. How lovely! How grateful I am!"

The second major shift occurred when I broke my humerus and spent over two months in a brace. As I've said before, I haven't exactly handled change gracefully or graciously. While I was laid up, I very definitely did not feel like myself. Yes, I was crabby at times before the accident, but my mood was more voluntary, if that makes sense. Yes, I was gloomy at times, but before my accident I could take some kind of action for distraction. And yes, I could lollygag about doing nothing before the enforced leisure, but lollygagging about when I could have or should have been doing something else was fun, a kind of guilty pleasure. After my accident, all these traits of mine became involuntary, a punishment to me (and certainly to others).

The third shift began when that brace disappeared after surgery. Finally, I was able to rebuild and renew and work toward being my old self. Make that a somewhat *changed* self. I never felt unsympathetic to people with physical challenges, but I feel a hell of a lot more sympathetic now.

I know I'm not unique. What are some of the changes in identity you have experienced—positive, negative, mixed, and whatnot? We all experience changes in our sense of identity at one time or another. Some are obvious, some we only notice over time, and some may never be known to us even though others notice them.

Always be wary of allowing someone else to define or determine your sense of identity. Yes, we can surely learn from the wisdom of others. I am always open—well, sometimes, anyway—to working on an improved me. But I am not open to having my identity *defined* by other people who think they know who I am or who I should become.

Remember the quote at the beginning of this chapter? I sing my own variation: "I am I, Helen Lambin, the Lord of La Mancha. (I can't think of a better title.) My destiny calls and I go!" You can use it too, if you wish to, because "You are *you*, _____, the _____! (Fill in your own name and identifier.) *Your* destiny calls and you go!"

9 CREATURES THAT COMFORT
Loss of a Pet

All things bright and beautiful, All creatures great and small,
All things wise and wonderful, The Lord God made them all.
                                        — Cecil Frances Alexander

"Don't feel so bad. You can get another. It was only a (dog, cat, bird, horse, hamster, bunny—circle one)." If you have just lost a beloved animal companion, these words don't offer much consolation.

No, it wasn't *only* a _____." It was a precious, healing, helping, beloved part of *your* life. Oh, yes, it was also a creature of God.

First this: God created the Heavens and Earth—all you see, all you don't see. Earth was a soup of nothingness, a bottomless emptiness, an inky blackness. God's Spirit brooded like a bird above the watery abyss. God spoke: "Light!" And light appeared. God saw the light was good and separated light from dark.... It was evening, and it was morning—Day One (Genesis. 1:1-5).

On the fifth day, according to the beautiful creation story in Genesis, God created sea creatures, fish, and birds. On the sixth day, God first said, "'Earth, generate life! Every sort and kind: cattle and reptiles and wild animals—all kinds...'" (Genesis 1:24-25). It was only later on that sixth day that we humans came along. From our beginning we were sharing our earth with animals—or, better yet, they were sharing it with us. While according to common translations we humans were given dominion or stewardship over the animals, some commentators point out that this means *responsibility for* and not *dominance of* earth's creatures.

Consider Luke's infancy narrative, the lovely story of Jesus' birth Luke uses to open his Gospel. Where is Jesus born? Not in an inn. Not in someone's home. He is born in a stable where Mary and Joseph had sought shelter for the night. He is wrapped in swaddling clothes and placed in a manger. And who—or what—is usually found around a manger? Animals.

Many Scripture scholars contend Luke was showing Jesus in this way as one of the have-nots who arrives among the have-nots: born in a stable, cradled in a manger, and first welcomed by shepherds, whose work was considered marginal. It makes sense, fitting in with Luke's ongoing theme of Jesus' concern for the poor and the marginalized, that is, the last who are *never* first.

I also like to think that this story shows Jesus, son of God, coming to share life not only among his fellow human creatures but also among others of God's creatures. Think of the figures in a typical Christmas crèche: Jesus, Mary, and Joseph, along with some sheep, often an ox, maybe a donkey, and other creatures, depending on the crèche designer. And who knows, maybe some of those sheep were the ones in the fields with the shepherds when they heard the angels announce Jesus' birth.

Call them pets. Call them animal companions. Call them four-footed or winged family members. For simplicity's sake, I'll call them pets. But don't believe anyone who says animals don't matter. They *do* matter. As anyone who has had and later lost a beloved pet knows first hand, they matter a lot. They give us their unconditional love, even if they do not always receive love from us. They love us in spite of our flaws, and they don't—and can't—point them out to us. They share our joy. They comfort us in times of sorrow and sickness. They do so for those they love, and they do the same for strangers, especially children.

Therapy dogs and even occasionally cats visit nursing homes, assisted living facilities, and other senior centers to interact with residents, to be held, and to give the gift of loving touch. A while back I met one of these therapy dogs, a little Shetland sheepdog belonging to Rev. Carl Dehne, SJ, then chaplain of a nursing home. The dog, like its owner, had genuine kindness in its nature. I would say "human" kindness, except that people don't have a monopoly on kindness. The dog was better behaved than some humans, but let's not get into that. The dog could bring warmth and dignity to a wheelchair-bound patient and greeted the healthy with playfulness.

Children learn gentleness and responsibility in helping care for a pet. They have fun, get some exercise, and learn how to help with training and caring for others. Kids find a source of comfort when they need comfort and have a "best friend" available when they most need it. (Yes, the same is true for adults.)

Pets, like humans, can also pay a price for their relationships. They grieve for lost human companions. Sometimes they have to put up with neglect, abuse, and abandonment. They are pretty much dependent on the whims of their human "owners." They share our circumstances, and sometimes they share our responsibilities. Think, for example, of the incredible work done by guide dogs, helper animals of various kinds, rescue dogs, and sometimes even ordinary dogs and cats.

When we adopted Fupzi, our third dog, she had one leg in a cast. She had evidently been abused at some point, might have been abandoned, and was living on the street when she was hit by a bus. She survived because of kindly anti-cruelty workers. At first she appeared depressed and anxious—with good reason, considering her probable past. She would lie on her blanket, quiet and listless. From the time Fupzi arrived, our beautiful big black cat Fridgie became her constant companion. Fridgie would go over to her blanket and curl up carefully against her. Then they would both go to sleep. Six years later Fupzi looked after Fridgie in his old age, caring for him as if he were her own child until he died.

Every one of our dogs, somehow knowing what time Henry, my husband, was due to come home from work, would wait at the window for him. After Henry's death, our dog Fupzi would wait outside the door of his room—wait for him to come home.

One of the reasons people may have difficulty sympathizing with those who have lost a pet is the misconception that pets can easily be replaced. They can't. Yes, you can eventually get another, and it may be a good idea to do so in time, but each pet has his or her own personality, just as we humans do. Some are incredibly tolerant, some more demanding, some are four-legged rocket scientists, some dumb as a box of rocks—and some of them can be the sweetest creatures ever born.

Of course you can't equate the loss of a pet with the loss of a human family member or extremely close friend. You can't go to a shelter and adopt a friend or relative. Wouldn't it be nice if we could? (By the way, if you are considering another pet, please, please, think of adoption. There are many wonderful animals in need of homes—for love, for comfort, for survival.)

The loss of a beloved pet is still a loss, and if it is *your* loss, *you* should be allowed to grieve without feeling foolish. If it is a friend's loss, your sympathy is an act of kindness—a kindness to the grieving owner and to yourself. Grieving the loss of a pet can broaden our understanding of compassion and the planet we share with all other creatures.

Oh, back to that little Sheltie belonging to Father Dehne. Unfortunately, the little dog became ill and died when he was only about eight years old, having brought happiness to a lot of patients and the chaplain along the way. Wanting to be helpful, I said, sincerely but somewhat tentatively, "I don't know what your beliefs are about this, but I believe your dog is in heaven." (And I do believe, whatever your definition of *heaven*.) The priest's answer was immediate and matter-of-fact, "Well, of course!" By sheer coincidence—or serendipity—I ran across a lovely visual of this in a *New Yorker* cartoon. Here a bearded, somewhat bewildered-looking but benign-appearing God is seated on his throne on a billowing cloud against a background of stars. On the same cloud, a small dog looks up, smiling and wagging his tail, as he places his ball at his Creator's feet.

10 MOVING ON
Broken Relationships

Breaking up is hard to do.
— Neil Sedaka and Howard Greenfield

Like love itself, broken relationships have been the subject of novels, po-
etry, plays, songs, films, television programs, and posts on social media.
But unlike love, there is nothing entertaining about broken relationships.
Not if you're directly involved, that is. And at least, not for quite some
time. It is often more painful for the break-ee, depending on the circumstances and the reasons, but depending on the circumstances and the reasons it can also be difficult for the break-er. Of course, it also depends on
the persons involved. Neil Sedaka recorded his song twice, once in 1962
and again in 1975, each time with a different arrangement and the same
timeless theme. No matter when, where, or why, some kind of break-up
is inevitable for each and every one of us.

The broken relationship may involve a lover, spouse, partner, or
even a good friend. It can vary widely in intensity, history, and complications, and can run the emotional gamut from high-school romance
to adult divorce. But whenever, however, wherever strong feelings are
involved, breaking up can be "hard to do"—even when it is the *best* thing
to do. Recovering from the hurt can be a challenge. We need to find a
way to grow *in spite* of the hurt and *because* of the hurt.

But, a word of caution here. I'm talking about what could be called
a normal or ordinary break-up. There are times when the broken relationship is anything but ordinary or normal, and can involve stalking,
assault, and even murder. If the break-up is with someone you're afraid
of or have reason to consider dangerous to you, to another, or to himself

or herself, don't mess around! Get appropriate help. If you need profes-sional help and legal help, get it. If you don't know where to start, talk to a counselor, a clergyperson, a lawyer, a doctor, or even a cop. Don't let yourself or anyone else be put in danger. Needless to say, you do not want to be the one who *becomes* or *is* a danger to others.

What we're talking about here is the much more ordinary and non-violent response to breaking up. There is no standard. Each break-up is individual and unique.

Take Jason, for example. We'll call him that because it is not his name. He is a composite. Jason likes women—on his terms. He likes them attractive, he likes them agreeable, and he likes them available—in every sense of the word. On the other hand, if they do make themselves avail-able, it diminishes them in his eyes, and he will joke with friends about his conquests. He often prefers women to appear no brighter than he is—definitely a challenge for him to find. He isn't violent. He goes along with the divorce arrangements, cares about his kids, and considers himself a good father. And in many respects he is, except—except—that his at-titude towards women spills over to his sons. In the long run this doesn't make for happiness for anyone. Attitude isn't everything, of course. Cir-cumstances are circumstances, but over time a change in Jason's outlook would certainly help him, his former spouses, and his children.

Or take Millie. She's a composite too. Her marriage had its prob-lems, but she has never been never able to fully recover from her divorce. It confirms her theory that men are unreliable, aren't really capable of love or fidelity, and are manipulators. Like Jason, Millie works at being responsible and cares about her kids. She considers herself a good parent, and in many respect she is, except—except—that her attitude toward men spills over to her daughters. Quite unintentionally, she encourages them to have either too much dependence or too much need for control—or sometimes both—in their relationships. This doesn't make for happiness for anyone.

Working out a different perspective on relationship breakups isn't easy, but doing so can be worth the struggle. *"Vale la pena."* It's the same in Spanish and in Italian, a rare coincidence. It's usually accompanied by a gesture of hands. *"Vale la pena."* That is, "It's worth the effort."

Take Janice, for example. She is a tall, attractive gray-haired woman who looks younger than her actual age, which is considerably younger than mine. She was devastated when her husband of nearly fifteen years requested a divorce. They had two daughters in grammar school to be considered. That made it difficult enough, but she also still loved her husband. A lot. It was even more devastating some time later when he told her he was remarrying—and did so shortly afterwards. So then what? Janice herself was the child of divorce, a very unpleasant one. Her well-to-do father had barely contributed to her support and never bothered to see her until she was an adult. She did not want things to be that painful for her children. She wanted and needed financial help in supporting her children, but she wanted them to have a relationship with their father and, later, their stepsiblings.

In addition, Janice did not want the pain of the broken relationship to dominate the rest of her life. It wasn't a quick process, and it wasn't easy, but she did move on, literally and figuratively. Once her daughters were grown, she found a job she finds rewarding in a city she finds fascinating. She has dated, but no, she isn't in a committed relationship. But if she were, it would be because she wants to be with that specific person. I'll always remember what she told her daughters about her situation. "Don't feel sorry for me," she said. "I loved your father, and we had a lot of happy years together. I have no regrets."

Incidentally, Janice's mother is now in a skilled nursing home, and one of the people who visited her recently? Her ex-son-in-law.

Each of us responds differently to stress and separation, loss, and transition. Tolstoy famously said, "Happy families are all alike; every unhappy family is unhappy in its own way." Just as every unhappy family is unhappy in its own way, so too each person in an unhappy relationship is unhappy in his or her own way. One size does not fit all. The point is to *move* through loss, not to become *mired* in it. No, I haven't been divorced, but I have experienced the loss of my husband after more than thirty years of marriage. I realize that the experience is not the same, because Henry did not to choose to leave me. Nor was there someone, as in another woman, to take my place. And yet, his death *did* make me feel as if someone else had taken my place. It *did* for a time make me feel diminished. It *did* affect family and friends. Thankfully, I did in a sense have to move on—not to put it all *behind me*, but to *bring along* what was helpful and healthy and *let go* of what was not.

Moving on is essential for all of the persons involved in a broken relationship. If there are children, it is even more essential. We don't want our children to bring *our* pain into *their* relationships.

It is also important to remember that after a breakup you are still *you*—not a lessened version, not a partial version of you. We have much to learn from broken relationships: things about ourselves we want to change and often can change, things we wish others could and would change. But there is also what I call the "some" factor. Some very nice people simply shouldn't be in a love relationship with each other. Some will eventually work things out better with someone else. And yes, some shouldn't be in a relationship with anyone at all. This last "some" may be happier single or may have too many complications in their own lives to share it intimately with others.

Break-up pain isn't always from the end of a romantic relationship. It can come when a valued friendship ends through argument, loss of contact, distance, betrayal, changed circumstances, for whatever reason or for no apparent reason. And again, there's obviously no one answer. Sometimes we need to try to mend the relationship and renew it. Sometimes we need to let it go. There are times when we need to speak up and say what's bothering us—after giving some thought to avoiding the I'm-having-a–bad-day-and-so-will-you syndrome. And there are also the magic words: "I am so sorry. I really screwed up." They can be applicable, if inelegant, in many, situations.

Remember, we are persons of value, people with gifts. The fact that love ends doesn't make us unlovable. Ultimately, we're the only persons who can do that.

11 SHIFT IN PERSPECTIVE
Dealing with *Really* Difficult People

I do not like thee, Doctor Fell,
The reason why I cannot tell;
But this I know, and know full well,
I do not like thee, Doctor Fell.
— Sir Thomas Brown

"Now, now, aren't you over-reacting?" *No, no, you don't understand.*

Most of us have or have had some difficult people in their lives. And many of us may have been the difficult people in other people's lives. Learning to deal with this reality is a part of life.

Nota bene! An important qualifier here. This chapter is *not* about dealing with an abusive relationship. That is a whole different situation in terms of health, law, safety, resources, and goals. If that is your situation or the situation of someone you know, please get help or help them get help. Speak with law enforcement personnel, counselors, clergypersons, wise friends. But please get help. Now.

Nor is this chapter about dealing with *ordinarily* difficult people or simply eccentric people. Some of my best friends are eccentric. In fact, most of my best friends are eccentric. They may even think I am too. In fact, I know they do!

What this chapter is about is dealing with *really* difficult people— people who seem to have a toxic effect on you and your life. The experience is painful, and the transition away from them can be difficult. These really difficult people may be colleagues, bosses, neighbors, family members, friends (or former friends), classmates, roommates, members of an organization you belong to, or even members of your faith community. No group is immune from the challenges of difficult people.

The key words here are *toxic effect*. We are not talking about the people who simply annoy us for a short time. These are the people who can leave you feeling off-balance, inadequate, angry, unappreciated, manipulated, and sleepless as you toss and turn at night, trying to figure out what to do. The term *really difficult* is not one size fits all. To paraphrase Tolstoy again, difficult people are difficult in their own way. And people react to them in different ways. Your toxic person or my toxic person may be someone else's new best friend.

Here are some basic variations—sort of like a rerun of eighth grade... or first grade. One is the Playground Bully, who controls through the abuse of power, perceived or real. Another is the Relentlessly Right, whose standards are so high no one can ever meet them—and who makes it evident that you don't. I'm sure you've also encountered the Always Right, the ones who *think* they are right, which of course is very annoying to those of us who actually *are*. Then there's the Offended Innocent, who dishes it out but cannot take it. For the Constant Competitor everything becomes a contest with the prize and rules undisclosed. For the Heat-Seeking Me-sile everything is self-referential. And finally, there are the People Who Simply Make Us Acutely Uncomfortable for reasons we can't quite understand.

I could give even more categories and a host of mixed categories. If we hold up one of those awkward reflective mirrors, we may even see ourselves in one or more of them. The titles may be mildly amusing—I hope they are—but the issue of dealing with difficult people isn't a joke. It can consume a lot of time, energy, feeling, and spirit, all of which could be better devoted elsewhere.

Whatever the form of their problems, dealing with really difficult people can overwhelm our lives, perspective, thoughts, and sometimes conversation. Their presence seems to brood over us while we brood about them—a never-ending loop. I can't offer any kind of all-purpose solution. Here again, one size doesn't fit all. We seek to handle this particular pain in an appropriate and constructive way, but in our own way, a way that flows from who we are.

I have learned a few tactics for dealing with really difficult people from my experience, the experiences of other people, literature, and yes, my faith. Here are a few things to try, things to avoid, and things in between.

First, homicide, literal or figurative, is *not* an option. It is illegal, immoral, and unhealthy all the way around. And if you are already feeling under-appreciated, your friends are not going to think better of you—unless you have some really strange friends. That being said, here are some ideas that may be helpful and are legal. They are not in order of importance.

- **Quitting and/or walking away.** This may be a good idea, a bad idea, a principled act, or simply childish. It depends on why we do it, how we do it, and how much thought we've given it. We may have an impulse to "show them," whoever they are, and make them sorry they didn't support us. This is a bad idea. They probably won't be sorry or at least not for long. Life will go on for them. If we to decide to move on, it should be because we think it is the *best* and the *right* thing for us to do. We have to be prepared to accept the negative as well as the positive consequences of doing so.

- **Brooding.** A certain amount of brooding is not only okay, but can also be useful. We're all human, and we need a chance to feel and process the pain or anxiety we're experiencing, but not indefinitely and not all the time. When the really difficult relationship starts taking over our thoughts, like a hamster on a wheel, that is too much. In that case brooding can just prolong the anxiety. One way to deal with this is in the following tip.

- **Asking ourselves why the person bugs us so much.** Is the problem related to our misinterpretation or over-reaction?

- **Talking things over with a wise friend or counselor.** This is a good idea. It doesn't mean talking things over with everyone we know. It does mean talking it over with someone whose judgment and discretion we trust, who values us, and who has values.

- **Distinguishing between their "bad behavior" and our "bad day."** This is often self-evident—afterwards. It's a good idea to figure it out first.

- **Anticipating triggers.** This involves reflection and reasoning, rather than brooding, although brooding may be involved. Difficult people, like the rest of us, have certain characteristic ways of behaving and certain things that really set us off. If we can see the triggers coming, we may be better able to see a way of responding so we don't simply react with anger or helpless silence, which often makes us even angrier.

- **Setting appropriate boundaries.** This can be difficult, but it is essential. It may involve some of the points above, such as talking it over with someone and anticipating triggers, and may take considerable reflection—and yes, even prayer.

- **Considering "to thine own self be true."** Shakespeare's Polonius may have been a duplicitous character, but his advice to Hamlet was on the mark. In dealing with someone we find really difficult, it is important not to fall into the trap of doing the very things we find so objectionable or becoming someone we don't want to be. See below.

- **Trying a different perspective.** As difficult as it may be to understand and accept, other people may find us just as annoying as we find them. Time to take another look in the mirror.

- **Keeping a sense of humor.** Yes it's a cliché, but laughter is good medicine, perhaps the best. The ability to laugh at ourselves and at the more absurd aspects of a situation can help us in keep things in perspective—and keep our sanity.

- **Praying.** Last but not least, we need to talk with God about our difficulty. Of course, the *with* involves listening as well. It may seem awkward to pour out our hearts, because it involves remembering that the person we find so difficult is also God's child, when what we really might like is for God to be equally annoyed with the person. The only problem with that is that if God were to be annoyed, God wouldn't be God, not one we could trust anyway. Our prayer could go something like this:

Lord, I know that X (the problem person) is your child, just as I am. And I understand that you love her/him just as you love me. But I am also having a hard time here, Creator and Creative God. I feel I am being treated unjustly and unkindly, and I don't know how to deal with it. I need your help—firsthand and second-hand. How do I change his/her behavior or change my response to it? How do I succeed in setting boundar-

ies and responding effectively without being unjust myself? Help me to put things in perspective and respond rightly. And while you're at it, could you please help your other child—the difficult one—learn something about dealing with others in a better way? Soon. And let that "better way" include, or especially be, me.

It may not bring any kind of immediate and perceptible change. But prayer can bring a kind of peace and new perspective. The other thing about prayer is that those persons we find so difficult could use our prayers too. They may not be all that happy with how things are going either. Being unhappy isn't an excuse for willfully making others unhappy, but it can be a catalyst for change.

Our faith perspective here, as elsewhere, gives us guidance, support, and a really astonishing context. Being a child of God *is* a big deal! We are all children of God, but being one doesn't insulate us against challenges—challenges from others or within ourselves. The athlete and evangelist Billy Sunday once said, "Going to church doesn't make us a Christian any more than going to a garage makes us an automobile." Becoming Christian is an individual project, a communal project, and a life-long learning and growing project—rather like learning what it means to be human. The Dalai Lama has said repeatedly that dealing with difficult people is an opportunity to learn compassion. Yes, that's the Dalai Lama speaking, and I think he has an edge on a lot of us. He certainly has one on me. But it does put rather a different spin on it all, doesn't it?

12 THE LABORER IS WORTHY OF HIRE
Loss of a Job

Hard and honest work earns a good night's sleep,
Whether supper is beans or steak. But a rich man's belly
gives him insomnia.

— Ecclesiastes 5:12

"I envy you! All that leisure time!"

Yes, the envied person has nothing to do except look for a job; send resumes; figure out how to put food on the table; pay the rent or the mortgage, unpaid bills, tuition, and transportation to find a new job; and try to arrange for affordable health insurance. Oh, yes, and maintain self-confidence and motivation. Wow, who wouldn't envy that? Don't misunderstand. I love leisure, but it should be voluntary, not imposed by the labor market. If it is involuntary, it is not leisure.

I am not making some kind of blanket statement about being rich or middle class, however that is defined. Another translation of the Bible uses the word *surfeit* in relation to the rich man's belly. According to *The American College Dictionary* surfeit is "the result of overindulgence, an excessive amount."

What I am saying is that losing a job isn't enviable. It's scary. It's depressing. It can diminish respect from others, and, perhaps worse, diminish our self-respect. It is certainly a challenge, and it can sometimes become opportunity, but it is not some kind of divine way to provide leisure time! When I broke my arm, it was suggested by well-intended but ill-advised persons that it was God's way of seeing that I got some rest in the midst of an active life. If so, I figured, God didn't know me very well.

I have lost jobs or been laid off. Many people have, especially in today's world. So I have a glimpse or how it feels. But, however real, it is only a glimpse. I was lucky enough to go through this in a very different time, a very different economy, a very different world. It was a world in which many believed that the laborer actually was worthy of his or her hire. Of course, there were and are those who don't believe every worker is worthy. That's where unions came in to speak and act on behalf of those who had little or no voice. Times have certainly changed.

I can't really say, "I *know* how you feel." I don't. I can only imagine. I have a good imagination, but I don't *know*. What I can and do know and feel is that my heart aches for the people who have lost their jobs, are unemployed, or are drastically under-employed. It aches for people I know. It aches for the ones I don't know. And it should.

"I envy you. All that leisure time." This is just one example of words intended to comfort but having the opposite effect. Good intentions can be sensitivity-challenged. Here are a few more examples.

"This is a golden opportunity." For the job seeker who has had no interviews after countless resumes have been sent out or no job offer after multiple interviews, this has a hollow sound. Yes, it can indeed be the beginning of something good. It may have been for others who have gone through it, and I certainly hope it will be for all who have been laid off or are radically under-employed. Remember the story of the laborers in the vineyard in Matthew? Some were job seekers who were the last to be hired after hanging about in the heat all day. They did okay at the end of the day, thanks to an honorable and humane employer, that is. (See Matthew 20:1-16.) But they still had to wait about without much hope—waiting, waiting to be called. The vineyard owner/employer was humane and recognized their situation. Yes, the vineyard owner was God, but aren't we all supposed to reflect God's care and concern?

"**Well, it wasn't much of a job anyway.**" Some people assume that for people working in lower-paying, lower-status jobs, such as retail or fast food (sometimes contemptuously referred to as "McJobs"), the loss of such a job is no big deal. Well, it *is* a big deal! These employees work hard, and they take pride in what they do. If they lose their jobs, it is still devastating, and they often have fewer resources to fall back on.

When a major bookstore chain closed, it was reported that some of the sales staff were weeping. I gather it was in private because one manager, most likely following orders from above, was observed directing employees to smile and be cheerful.

I'm retired from my former full-time job, but not retired from writing. But here's the difference: I *chose* retirement, and I was fortunate enough to *have* a choice. For anyone, or at least most people who experience it in this day and age, unemployment can be traumatic, frightening, and demoralizing. It most certainly is not enviable.

If you are among the unemployed, I am truly sorry. You and all who are in this position are in my prayers. This chapter is dedicated to the unemployed, but is also written for those who may not even know them, those who have the power to create or take away jobs. We'll get to them in a little bit. Meanwhile, if you are in this painful transition, here are a few suggestions.

First of all, hold on tightly to hope. Hope doesn't make things happen. Finding a job takes work—most of it unpaid. It can take help from others—like us. Giving up hope can lead to giving up altogether—a self-fulfilling prophecy. Being unemployed does not—repeat, *does not*—

make you less of a valued, valuable person. It makes you a person under more stress, but it does not—repeat, *does not*—make you less of a person.

If you are not unemployed or don't know anyone who is, you're not off the hook. We all have a part to play in solving the problems contributing to high unemployment: globalization, robotization, corporate greed, and individual selfishness. All of us have to do our part, "for the laborer deserves three square meals" (Luke 10:7).

One of the things we hear from pointy-headed pundits is that some Americans just don't want to work. They rail against unemployment benefits, claiming those benefits are a reward! Oh, yeah. Oh, yeah. This is a response lacking not only in compassion but also in common sense—and accuracy. Yes, there will always be some people who don't want to work. And there will also people who are unable to do full-time work because of physical or mental limitations. It's called disability. Generally speaking, however, people consider it inhumane to starve the sick and cast them out on the street.

For the most part, however, people do want to work. They wouldn't line up in the rain by the hundreds or thousands at dawn for a handful of jobs if they didn't. If you or someone you know is or has been recently unemployed, you know what I'm talking about: the toll it takes on individuals and their families, the difficulty of clinging to hope, and the courage it takes to keep on trying.

So what can we—we, the people—do to help? I am not an expert in this field. Or most fields. But here are a few suggestions.

- Think of the common good. It is called the *common* good because it is better for *everyone*. An economy where economic benefits are widely shared and the poor and sick are cared for is a stable one. One with wide economic disparity is not. Just recall history.

- Stop making it rewarding to outsource jobs. Yes, outsourcing can make goods cheaper to buy here, but quality can suffer. Just watch the news about product safety and durability—or lack of it Should there really be tax breaks for doing this? And if no one is working, who can afford to buy even the less expensive products?

- Oppose union busting. Unions are not perfect. No institution is. But unions have helped improve quality of life for millions upon millions of people. Opponents sometimes say, "I don't belong to a union, so how has it benefited me?" Well, who do you think worked to get the benefits you *do* have? They didn't drop down from corporate America like manna from heaven.

- And speaking of corporate America.... Yes, it has certainly brought benefits, but we humans, including members of corporate America, are imperfect. Corporate America needs regulations, checks, and balances...just as unions do.

- One percent of Americans should not control twenty-five to forty percent of the wealth. This needs no explanation.

- All voices in a democracy need to be heard. While money talks, it shouldn't drown out everything else. Democracy is not a commodity.

- When even economists cannot define or explain some financial high-wire acts like derivatives of derivatives, we have a problem. We shouldn't need computers capable of accomplishing 70,000 financial trades per second. Investment should create jobs, products, and services, not just a hell of a lot of money for a few.

- And about service.... Some employment theorists say that we are going to become a service economy. If so, then we need to see that service work is respected and decently paid, with guaranteed benefits.

- Health care should be a guaranteed benefit. It should be available to the disabled, those laid off, and the retired. It should be sensibly administered and include preventative care. And it could help in creating jobs, instead of destroying them, because...

- A number of people who are entrepreneurially gifted, but afraid to leave jobs currently providing their health insurance, could start their own businesses and eventually provide employment for others.

- At this point in time, we only have one planet that can sustain life as we know it. Since we need to do some repair and clean up work, we could and should create jobs in the environment, in infrastructure, in developing ways to live in community, and in promoting sustainable agriculture.

- We worry, legitimately, about the deficit. Well, one of the big, big contributors to the deficit is war. Working on diplomatic solutions is a better economic option than sending our young off to be killed or severely injured. Diplomacy is less costly in lives, quality of life, gifts, energies, and yes, money.

- Controversy arises a lot these days whenever anyone suggests more equitable distribution of income. Well, what do these speakers think Jesus of Nazareth was talking about? And what about prophets like Amos, who, speaking for

God, had this to say? "Do you know what I want? I want justice—oceans of it. I want fairness—rivers of it. That's what I want. That's *all* I want" (Amos 5:24).

Remember, the laborer really is worthy of his or her hire. We need to respect the dignity of all honest labor and recognize the universal desire for a living-wage job. Finally, it is a good thing to remember these words: "We hold these truths to be self-evident, that all men are created equal, that they are endowed by their Creator with certain unalienable Rights, that among them are Life, Liberty, and the pursuit of Happiness." They are from the Declaration of Independence, of course, echoing down through the years since 1776.

Let's make a good start on building a better world by trying to live the ideas contained in this document today as best we can.

13 WHAT, THEN, IS HEALING?
Changes in Health

Are there no healing ointments in Gilead? Isn't there a doctor in the house? So why can't something be done to heal and save my dear, dear people?
— Jeremiah 8:22

Throughout the year in our faith communities, we pray for the sick, whether they are members of our churches or not. We do so during worship, and we do so on our own. We also do so in small groups. We don't necessarily specify just what we are praying for on their behalf but, articulated or otherwise, we usually include prayers for support, for hope, and for caregivers. We also include prayers for healing. Some of the people we pray for get better, and some do not. For some there may be little or no change for the better, and some may have illnesses that lead to death. So what then *is* healing?

It can be hard to know how to respond when someone is sick, whether that person is a family member, friend, or even ourselves. Illness changes life, temporarily or on a much longer-term basis, for the person who suffers and for everyone involved. It's natural to try to find reasons for the illness—to reassure ourselves, to comfort others. In many circumstances, we can certainly do things to improve our over-all health—think nutrition and exercise for openers—but usually it isn't all that simple.

I have thus far—I am almost afraid to write it—been "lucky." (I am part Welsh and mixed Celt among my multiple ancestral roots. So I am therefore superstitious about saying anything too positive about the future.) My health has been remarkably good although I have a few health issues. And certainly I have had loved ones who were ill. So what I offer here is based on my gratefully-limited experience.

All illnesses are not created equal—not in level of discomfort or pain, not in degree of seriousness, not in prognosis, and not in cost. When people face illness without health insurance or access to adequate care, they often face economic hardship as well

Health—good, bad, and in between—is, in part, a lottery. Some of my own family and friends are examples. My maternal grandmother died at ninety-three. Her oldest son and youngest daughter both died at ninety-five, but her youngest son died at fifty-six of a heart attack. My Grandfather Reichert died at ninety-three when he fell from a barn roof he was repairing. Actually, the fall didn't kill him, but lying in bed and catching pneumonia did. As a young adult, his granddaughter Vera survived non-paralytic polio. Now a senior, she has had four recurrences of Non-Hodgkin's lymphoma, receiving five rounds of chemotherapy—with residual damage from the chemo. She wishes now that the oncologist had been more specific about the consequences of that much chemo. The oncologist's response was, "Well, you're alive, aren't you?" Yes, she is, but she would liked to have been able to make a more informed choice. We all have the right to make informed choices.

My friend's son Chris was a firefighter honored by the city of Chicago for his life-saving (and life-risking) professional dedication. Chris died at forty-six, not through work-related dangers, but from the invasion of cancer. A beloved niece, Therese, died of cancer one year after celebrating her fiftieth birthday. Young children face death as well. Illness is indifferent to age.

So, small wonder that we try to find answers for things that cannot yet be answered. And small wonder we sometimes do not know how to respond. "Maybe this is God's way of seeing that you got some rest from your demanding job." Someone actually said that to the young woman who had a double mastectomy shortly after being laid off from her job. Say what? The comment was no doubt well intended, but, I repeat, say what? I do not think God sent her or anyone else cancer. But God certainly did not send the woman cancer so she could get some rest.

On a rainy Easter Sunday night in 2010, I fell down the back steps of my house and broke my humerus. As a result, I spent just over ten weeks in an immobilizer, a plastic brace that held my arm in place at right angles with Velcro straps and metal fasteners that crossed my body. I could have had surgery, but chose instead to try to see if it would heal naturally. (I was told this could take about twelve weeks.) It definitely was immobilizing, and it was definitely not fun, but people with the kindest of intentions suggested the "rest" perspective, implying that God sent the injury so I could get a break from my rather active life. I don't think so. If that were true, God doesn't know me very well. And I think God probably knows me all too well.

Eventually I wound up having surgery anyway since, after ten weeks, the arm still wasn't healing properly. So I have a titanium rod and four screws in my left arm. Fortunately, it isn't noticeable now to me or anyone else.

I would *like* to tell you that I handled those weeks with grace and fortitude and good humor. I would *like* to say that, but I can't. I was a terrible patient! I frankly don't know how anyone was able to stand me. I could barely stand myself. All of a sudden, I had become someone else, or at least a different version of me. With "The Fall," I fell into profound depression—albeit reactive or situational depression, but depression nevertheless. I recognized it for what it was. And I knew what kind it was. My husband, Henry, was a psychologist, and some of his knowledge rubbed off on me by osmosis, I guess. But this knowledge didn't help me deal with the pain. As Howell, one of those loyal friends who put up with me during that period, put it, "You were like an angry cat." I was. (For all you cat lovers out there, don't be offended. I am one of you. Cats have shared their home with us for more than forty years. But have you ever tried to medicate or deal with a pissed-off cat?)

"Is there anything at all you look forward to?" That's what Pastor Monte Johnson asked on one of the occasions when he came to my home to bring me communion. It was a good question.

"Nothing," I said—or rather growled. "Absolutely nothing."

By day I waited for night when the day would be over. By night I waited for dawn when the night would be over. I wouldn't exactly call that *looking forward*, or even *waiting*, in the best sense of the word.

If I were asked that question by my pastor now, I might answer in a somewhat similar fashion, perhaps without the growl, but for a very different reason. Today I am grateful for the ordinariness of life. During the Immobilizer Period, I had to try to shower wearing plastic garbage bags over the brace, and baths were out of the question. One of the first things I did after the brace was off, while the left arm was still very weak, was have a dress rehearsal for a lovely hot bath. I crawled into an empty tub fully dressed (minus shoes) in shorts, shirt, and undergarments. I wanted to be ready in case someone had to call the fire department to extract me. They didn't. And learned I could at last soak in a bath.

Now, some four years later, I still don't have absolutely full motion in my arm, but it is very close to a normal range, and I am still working on it. But to have *almost* full motion and to be able to do the things again I could do before the break? Three years ago this seemed like a squandered dream. Let's hear it for ordinariness!

The time in the brace was a long ten weeks, and I loathed every minute of it. It was most definitely not—repeat, *not*—in the same category of loss and difficulty of major illness and disability, but it gave me a glimpse of how those might feel. My discomfort was temporary, not chronic. It was not life threatening. So, no, I don't *know* how it feels to be really sick or disabled. To try to draw a comparison would be absurd and unfair. What I do know from my experience and that of others is that coping with serious illness demands extraordinary courage, endurance, patience, and hope. It can require extraordinary resources, both inner and outer, both on the part of those who are ill and their caregivers, friends, and families.

And what I do know—or at least believe—is that this is one time God *can* say, "I know how you feel." Not only as the all-knowing, all-understanding God, but as the human face of God we know as Jesus of Nazareth. His sufferings were compressed in terms of time—days or hours, not months or years. But they were indeed horrific in their pain and fear, intensity and humiliation. So when we are told God is with us and can understand the fear, pain, loneliness, sorrow, and sense of loss of dignity that come with major illness? Yes, God can and does understand.

Four years after the pastor asked what I looked forward to, I now have an answer. Yes, I *do* look forward to things, biggish things (occasionally) and smaller things (a lot), but I try not to look forward too much—not because of the depression that made me want to get this day, this night, this month over with, but because of my new-found gratitude for *this* day. "Don't wish your life away," my mother used to say when I was little and expressed my impatience for things like Christmas, birthdays, or summer vacation. I didn't understand then. I certainly do now. I try not to wish my life away. I enjoy this day. *This* day. I try to be present to the moment. Buddhism emphasizes this, and it is a valuable insight not just for Buddhists, but for us Christians as well. On Easter we say, "This is the day the Lord has made. Let us rejoice and be glad." *That* day, following death and celebrating resurrection, is meant to be part of *every* day, *every* life.

14 THE FACE IN THE MIRROR
Changes in Appearance

You, darling, you look absolutely marvelous.
— Billy Crystal

The words of Billy Crystal's comic song are often paraphrased as "You look mahvelous, dahling." Nice ring to them, isn't there?

As we advance in age, grace, and wisdom, our skills and perspective advance…and so does our appearance. Now and then we can be startled when we look in the mirror. "Mirror, mirror, on the wall. Can that really be me at all?" (The quote is my own.)

I don't look like I did when I was twenty or thirty or forty. Actually, I don't look like I did when I was sixty. I recently came across a black and white photo taken of me in my twenties. I'm on a beach in a black one-piece swimsuit. Short dark hair, no wrinkles. *Hey, I look pretty good—except for the cigarette I'm holding.* (I stopped smoking some years ago.) In the hall there's a color photo of me with the children when they were young—and I was too, approaching thirty-nine. (The *actual* thirty-nine, not the one I claimed to be for years.)

I look at another picture on the wall. Long dark hair, peasant blouse, no observable wrinkles, or only a few anyway, and more compact horizontally, for want of a better word. And I sigh. As another song said: "Those were the days, my friend. We thought they'd never end…." But of course they did. Or underwent radical change. My beloved husband, Henry, who took both pictures, has passed on. I hope he is happy somewhere even more beautiful than the beach and the lake in those photos. His absence still leaves a hole that can be walked around and beyond, but still can't be filled, any more than you can fill a hole in the sand with water.

My appearance has changed. The dark hair is gray—well, actually white. In some cultures gray hair is a sign of wisdom, but that is generally not the case in our society. I don't know that I've yet acquired that much wisdom, but I'm working on it. There are some lines there—frown lines, laugh lines, miscellaneous lines. And my face is rounder. Along with the years have come some twenty pounds. On good days when I look in the mirror, I see a less distinguished version of my mother's face. On not so good days, I think: How did I get to *be* Mom?

Cover girl I never was. But still, she looks rather attractive, that girl, that woman in the photos. Do I miss looking like I once did? Damn right I do.

If next week I could have some kind of uber-cosmetic procedure that would restore me to looking as I did forty some years ago, would I do it? Now that's a different question. The answer is no, not really. Is this surprising? Actually, it rather surprised me at first, but how I *appeared* then was part of who I *was* then, not who I *am* now. Do I really want to have people expect me to have the same energy I had at forty? Do I really want to lose some of the wisdom and perspective that years, experience, and judgment—good and bad—have brought?

Actually, I do have a role model in the type of confident, elegant, acerbic Englishwoman played by the actress Maggie Smith in films and TV shows like *Downton Abbey*. I'm not as confident as she is, and I'm much less elegant. But I can be as acerbic.

Men have somewhat of an edge in this aging process. Think of the status in the media, and often in life, of a nice-looking, gray-haired bachelor. Nevertheless, men also have the same experience in looking at old photos. At least I hope they do!

Try this sometime. At a social gathering, ask people how old they actually are on the *inside*. I've tried it with both women and men, and the results have been interesting. (Full disclosure here. For "some years" I've been twenty-four—the year I met my future husband. This doesn't discount my children and granddaughter. I wouldn't give them up for the world—even if I am only twenty-four.)

But as far as that face—and figure—in the mirror.... What are we willing to do? We can take measures to look our best. We can work at having a healthy diet and appropriate exercise for health and quality of life as well as appearance. We can find a clothing style that fits our style with an individual touch—a colorful scarf here, a striking shirt there. Fortunately my own style is not upscale.

But, when that cosmetological fairy godmother appears to offer the instant change with five-year warranty, I think I'll answer no. What about you?

That face in the mirror? That is me. Now. Today. It is who I am, and, if there is anything I really really dislike, it's trying to pretend to be something or someone I'm not.

Anyway, remember: Billy Crystal had it right. To paraphrase him slightly, "Dahling, you *still* look mahvelous."

15 DISTANCE LEARNING
Changes in Community

Those were the days, my friend, We thought they'd never end,
We'd sing and dance forever and a day….
>   — Gene Raskin

The words above are from a song with international roots and universal appeal. It is based on the melody and lyrics of a Russian folk song, and it was made popular by both French singer Edith Piaf and Welsh singer Mary Hopkin. In many ways, those lyrics speak to me. Those *were* the days, and I miss them dearly. Sometimes I miss them in the middle of the night—well, maybe not the part about the singing and dancing forever and a day. But I do miss the expansive sense of community I once enjoyed. At my age, that expansive community has radically changed.

I began writing this chapter one night at 3:20 a.m. because I couldn't sleep. When I can't sleep, sometimes I read or think—or write. That one night I was thinking specifically of all those communities I used to be a part of—*used to be* being the significant verb. Now, some months later, I'm revising this, and it's afternoon, but the "3:20 a.m. feeling" still persists. But going back to those expansive communities. Some existed at the same time, some at different times, and included:

- my original family, including my extended family
- school friends
- the Lambin nuclear family—my husband and the kids

- neighborhood friends, many of whose kids had also grown up here
- the "lunch bunch" at work at various jobs
- the liturgy team at my former Catholic parish
- two renewal or faith-sharing groups at two different churches
- the long-time friends of my husband who also became my friends
- miscellaneous friends, very important but not easily categorized
- members of a decade-long book group
- our dogs and cats

My husband died. Friends passed away, one just this year. Kids moved on. Friends moved away to Florida, St. Louis, and elsewhere. Neighbors moved to suburbs. I retired. I joined another church. I got careless about calling people, including long-time friends, because I was always hoping for a better moment. Our pets died too, but we now have a secondhand grand-dog. (He is rather large and somewhat strong, and I am rather small and somewhat senior. Dog-walkers hired by his parents come several times a week.) Even the book group finally fell apart. Communities ended or changed for a variety of reasons—not with a bang, often with not even a whimper—but change they did. Where did everybody go?

Yes, I know. In many ways I am lucky. I have great kids and a granddaughter whom I not only *love* dearly, but whom I actually *like*. And they love me too. Thank God. I include their spouses and significant others in that embrace. I also include my nieces, nephews, Missouri in-laws, and Iowa cousins. In some cases, we may rarely see one another because of time and distance, but we know we are there for one another.

I am lucky enough to still have good friends—new and old. (If you are reading this, you all know who you are. And I'm damn glad for your presence.)

I have good people who share my home. My daughter Rosemary, who is on disability due to health problems, lives here, as does her significant other, Skip. Rosemary is witty, kind, and enjoyable to live with, and I like Skip. It can be good having a man in the house.

But there are things I miss. Like the drop-ins of close neighborhood friends. I could just show up at their home for coffee. or they could show up at mine. I enjoyed being part of a defined or semi-defined group and sharing the sense of group identity that allowed me to just show up and people were happy to see me. And if I didn't show up, people wondered why I wasn't there and wished I was.

As I said earlier, I miss being someone's Number One Person, specifically Henry's Number One Person. My kids each have their own Number One. That has always been one of the big wishes Henry and I had for our children: that as they reached adulthood each would find a Number One Person.

The late great Bette Davis famously said, "Old age is no place for sissies." I don't know about that. Too many people don't have the opportunity to grow old because of early illness, accident, or violence. So I appreciate the opportunity, but I personally find the thought of growing old scary at times, especially in the context of shrinking communities. Of course, I mean the thought of growing old in the *future*. Right now, at the age of eighty-one, I don't consider myself actually old, just experienced.

When I started working on this book, I learned that my younger daughter Jeanne and her husband Scott might be moving to Hong Kong.

Scott would be teaching photography at the Hong Kong branch of an American college. I may as well admit it. I was temporarily devastated. I even prayed for what was best for them, but hoped that "the best" would be closer to here, or at least on this continent. Well, Hong Kong won. It's not that I thought they shouldn't make the move. Hong Kong, I've heard, is a beautiful and fascinating city, and given the chance I might well have moved to some distant exotic location myself when I was younger. But I am not their age by more than thirty years, and, as the person who would be left behind, expected the separation to be much more difficult for me than it would be for them.

The Hong Kong branch of the family and I always have the opportunity for contact by phone, by email, and in person, but staying in contact has become considerably more complex. Yet Jeanne and Scott are *still here* in this world. Anyone who has experienced separation or lost a loved one knows what *still here* means. It means I have had to do what I call "Distance Learning," that is, learning or relearning how to bridge distances to those we love who have moved away from our own community or have moved from an easily-accessible location to an inaccessible one.

I was going to call this chapter "Loss of Community," but thought better of it. Loss may or may not be applicable in all situations, but change most certainly is. I said above that change is inevitable if you live long enough, meaning that we have to keep on learning to live with change—changes we enjoy, changes we don't. So, what are some of the ways of dealing with changes in community? Each of us has our own way. But here are a few thoughts I had—at 3:20 a.m. and at 3:20 p.m.

- If the loss is from simple attrition, that is, lack of follow-up on our part, we can try to do better. I am very bad about making phone calls to friends or potential friends. I think about it. I intend to do it. And then somehow I don't get around to it. Something as simple as keeping in touch might help rebuild a little community.

- If we "fall out" with one or more persons in a given community, can we "fall back in"? Should we? Do we want to? If so, what kind of words or actions will help? And if someone else makes the first gesture, how do we respond?

- Change may involve learning to enjoy doing some things on our own—going to a movie, dining out, or traveling alone or with a tour group. It can involve reading, writing, playing an instrument, or participating in some kind of sport. When we engage in these kinds of activities for our own good, we increase our level of self-sufficiency. But it's also good for relationships and for the community. After all, if we can't enjoy being around ourselves, how can we expect others to?

- We need to be open to new friends and new communities. Old friends are wonderful, but new friends can be too. Some of my newer friends, like some of my older ones, are definitely younger than I am. Actually, at my age, a lot of people—in fact, most—are younger than I am!

- We have to make an effort to move on, up, or out. Sometimes it is a matter or simply moving on. I have, at different times, been both the mover-on and the moved-on for want of better words. It can be hard to feel we are left behind or out, and it can be hard to decide when it is time to move on ourselves. When I'm in this spot, I try to apply reflection, reason, and prayer—all to be able to respond appropriately, with grace and good judgment.

- And speaking of prayer, that leads to another vital part of the relational equation: We are not alone even when we are alone. The fact is, if we live long enough, we are going to outlive some of those we have loved, liked, or loathed. Some of the people who loved me unconditionally have passed on. My father, my mother, my husband. Others who loved me, even if not unconditionally (and you can't always expect that), have as well. In one sense, cherished friends and neighbors are now part of the past, but in another sense they are still with me along with the other known and unknown cast of characters that we Christians call the Communion of Saints.

- And beyond, beneath, giving life and spirit and love to that Communion, is God. God is there. God is here. A living, loving presence.

To me, living, loving, and aging all involve faith. (More about this in "Now Where Did I Leave It? Loss of Faith.") I know people who grow old gracefully and graciously without faith, but I have a hard enough time growing old graciously *with* it. I cannot imagine growing old *without* it. Not just because of what comes next, but because of what comes *now*—God with you, and God with me. God is with us when we are with others, and God is with us even when we are alone or feel most alone. God is with us amidst noise and busy-ness and confusion. And God is with us in the silence at 3:20 a.m. And at 3:20 p.m.

Oh, and back to that move to Hong Kong. When your child gets married, the saying is, "You're not losing a daughter. You're gaining a son." Or vice versa. It's a good thought and a consolation in my present situation. We are not temporarily losing a daughter and son-in-law. We are temporarily gaining their rather large and very lovable black dog, Aldo, and their small cat, Harvey. It wasn't intended as a trade, of course, but here are two new pets forming a new animal community with my two cats. Aldo is getting up there in years, a little gray around the muzzle and a little stiff in the joints. I understand. I am already also very gray and a little stiff. We will make a nice pair, strolling hand in paw into the sunset years together. Ah, community!

16 LAUGHTER AND TEARS AND…
Perspective on Perspective

When you do find humor in trying times, one of the first and most important changes you experience is that you see your perplexing problems in a new way—you suddenly have a new perspective on them.

— Allen Klein

All right, the words above may be something of an overstatement. Some situations strongly resist humor, but humor can also be a saving grace. Often it may not take away the pain, but it may make it more bearable, especially when it comes to how we feel about ourselves and others.

When I was about thirteen, I began to realize that other kids were laughing at me—not a happy discovery. Not only that, I didn't understand why and certainly was not about to ask. What if someone answered! After mulling it over for a while, I came up with a solution of sorts. If I laughed *first*, then they couldn't actually laugh *at* me. Could they? Well, they still could, of course, but I would feel differently about it. So I soon learned how to laugh at myself.

In the process, I also learned something else: that I had a moderate talent and a definite taste for making other people laugh. Take, for example, the Senior Class Show. All the other senior girls wore formals for the song they would sing together, "A Pretty Girl Is Like a Melody." Not me. I appeared in a reprise of a skit on courtship from freshman year—when I played the Cave Woman. Instead of a formal, I wore two gunnysacks, fashionably tied with a rope around my waist, was bare-footed, sported a smear of mud on my face, and was dragged happily off stage by my Cave

Man co-star. For a brief moment, I thought it might have been nice to be one of those melody-pretty girls in a formal. But not for long. There it was: the now-sweet sound of an auditorium full of laughter. *At* me, yes, but also *with* me. It was music to my ears.

I'm not suggesting that we should all go out and buy clown suits. But what I learned is that sometimes situations and events that seem disappointing or uncomfortable at first can teach us something we might have taken much longer to learn—like being laughed at in eighth grade and being able to laugh at myself at eighty. If you plan to grow old, or grow old without much planning, a sense of humor is going to help along the way. For us. For those around us.

I am not talking here about many of those so-called "funny" emails about aging. Most of them aren't funny to me. Yes, aging has its funny side. Life does. But too many of those emails and posts on social media offer a canned look at aging focusing on memory loss, incontinence, drooping flesh, arthritis, hearing loss, vision loss, loss of common sense, and problem private parts. You get the picture. Or if you're lucky, maybe you don't and won't. It could be that my sense of humor is peculiar. It very likely is. So if those images float your boat, okay, but just don't send them to me.

Laughter can be loving, sympathetic, cruel, callous, smart, stupid, and everything in between, although I'm not sure cruelty or callousness should qualify as true laughter. I will define *true laughter* as soon as I figure out how to define it. Or maybe not. It is not easy to define. Humor can help us recognize the difference between the way things are supposed to be and the way things really are. But, more than that, laughter can help us accept life in this imperfect world. Our world doesn't need to be perfect. Life would be boring if it were. We just need our world to be livable, with joy and sorrow and hope for all.

What I *do* know is that if we plan to grow old—and even if we don't plan—laughter can be a valuable part of our "maturing" perspective, if you want to call it that. What I'm talking about is what I call *creative laughter*: laughter that has some originality and compassion, laughter that brings a breath of fresh air, or maybe a breath of the Spirit.

Why are tears included in the title of this chapter? Because they are part of the picture too. We generally come into the world crying and are going to do some of it—and sometimes a lot of it—along the way. Sometimes we shed visible tears, that is, tears that can be seen by others. Sometimes, we cry invisible tears, tears on the inside, hidden from others and, at times, even from ourselves.

A caveat here. I am not talking about Tears-as-a-Negotiating-Technique. We have probably all encountered people who cry to *appear* very vulnerable when they don't get their own way. Small children eventually grow out of this phase, but occasionally adults carry it with them through life. Sure, it can produce results, but it can also produce resistance and withdrawal. Think of some examples in classic movies, like Anne Baxter's character in *All About Eve*. Or think of the fable "The Boy Who Cried Wolf."

What I am talking about is tears—real tears, visible or invisible. We cry from grief, and we cry from other pain, physical and emotional. We cry from regret. We cry for others, and we can even cry from laughter. We can cry from imagination and identification, for example, when we choke up during a film.

I tend to be one of those invisible weepers. It's not a matter of principle. My sorrow just doesn't necessarily manifest itself in external waterworks. On the other hand, I can choke up at a good film or TV show or even a particular piece of music.

Tears, however they are manifested, can be healing. They can elicit compassion and demonstrate compassion. If laughter fertilizes the soil of growth, tears water it. Even Jesus wept. (See Luke 19:41 and John 11:33-35.)

Someone might point out that Scripture does not say that Jesus laughed, but I would say that just because it doesn't say so, doesn't mean it never happened. Think of Peter leaping from the boat confidently to walk on the water, and then...glug-glug-glug..."Help!" (See Matthew 14:22-33.) Do you think Jesus didn't laugh at some point at Peter's embarrassing rescue? Or what about the Wedding Feast of Cana when everyone was exclaiming about the quality of the newly introduced wine—the wine Jesus had made from water after his mother told him to. (See John 2:1-11.) I suspect there are any number of times when Jesus laughed. To be fully human, I submit, includes having a sense of humor. Remember, Jesus' charisma drew people to him from far and wide. It is hard to imagine a charismatic teacher without a sense of humor.

As Christians, we believe that Jesus was not only fully human but fully divine. Does this mean that God has a sense of humor? What do *you* think?

17 TATTOO THIS!
Growing Improbably Older

But the odd thing was that one never felt old. She always felt that she was twenty-five, not a day more or a day less, but, of course, one couldn't expect other people to agree to that.

— Virginia Woolf

The quotation above from *The Voyage Out* expresses the unspoken feelings of a seventy-two-year-old woman as she stands at a gate on a country road, talking to a young couple in love. I love it. It expresses my own feelings exactly, except that I think of myself as *twenty-four*, not a day more or a day less! I ran across this quote some years back, absorbed it, then I forgot where I found it, and looked for it off and on for five years without success. I finally found it—near the end of the novel—when I had almost given up looking.

Virginia Woolf was a novelist and essayist, not a gerontologist, but I think she had it right. I couldn't have said it more precisely myself. I am twenty-four—inside, that is, but of course I cannot expect other people to agree to that. There can be, for many of us, maybe most of us, a disconnect between our chronological age and our *real* age, that is, our perceived age.

In an earlier chapter I recommended a non-game I use when friends gather—friends who are grown up, at least legally. It's worth repeating. Ask each person how old he or she is *inside*. You'll notice that the inside ages can be a little, or a lot, different from the chronological ages. Answers can range from several decades younger than the actual age to close to it. Rarely do people pick their current age or older! My answer in the non-game has usually been twenty-four. That was the year I met my husband one day in May. I remember earlier that spring sitting on an el platform, waiting for the train to come, feeling: "Something good is going to happen to me." And it did.

Now that you have read this far, however, we're sort of old friends, so okay, I'll admit I have added some additional years. This year I have turned—oh, help, yikes—eighty-one!

Until my age was outed—with my permission—on TV in 2011, I didn't really admit how old I was. I had concealed my age for so long from other people that I had concealed it from myself. By implying, believably or otherwise, that I was in my sixties, I had come to believe it myself. So it was a bit of a shock to realize that I was actually seventy-eight at the time. You could say that I aged overnight!

Turning forty, fifty, sixty, and even seventy? Piece of cake. Okay, it wasn't quite a piece of cake. There was that tattoo.... But still, it wasn't *eighty!* (If you are reading this and turning ninety or one hundred, my apologies for whining. If you are only turning forty, fifty, sixty, or so, lighten up, kids. Let's talk.)

The way the "outing" happened was this. For my seventy-fifth birthday, I got my first tattoo. I had been afraid I was growing old gracefully and decided to do so instead a little disgracefully. That first tattoo was a lovely peace daisy, high on the upper left arm, where I could reveal it or conceal it as it fit my mood. Of course, I didn't know then it was going to be the first tattoo of what would prove to be...well, never mind. Exact numbers don't necessarily give a true picture. Let's just say that the picture became part of a gallery. And no, I have no regrets about what I started.

One reason the tattoos have meaning for me is that they have *permanence*. Over a lifetime there are a lot of changes, welcome and unwelcome. Just when you think you begin to understand something quite well, some kind of *Version 3 of Whatever* comes along. But once the tattoos are there, they are *there*. Yes, they can fade some over time, but they bring a sort of a sense of completion.

A more important reason for the tattoos has to do with community—a changeable one, but a community nevertheless. The ink has become a bridge—a bridge that crosses barriers of race, age, gender, ethnicity, culture, location, and class. Because of the tattoos, I wind up talking with a wide variety of people—nice people, interesting people, people of widely different backgrounds, situations, and stories. The conversations may take place on public transit, on the streets, in stores, and in restaurants, but many are with people who, in ordinary circumstances, wouldn't be interacting with me. I am a "mature" woman living in a big city of several million people. How can we bridge the gap of the unknown and anonymity? And how can we recognize the bonds we share? Having good tattoos gives me a conversational bridge. (By *good* I mean not only quality artwork but a quality message—a positive and thoughtful or funny symbol, not one deliberately meant to offend.)

I'm certainly not advocating that everyone should rush out and get a tattoo. This is a highly individual choice, not to everyone's taste or comfort level. (If for any reason you actually decide to get inked, make sure you go to an established, reliable, regulated shop.) But what I do think we need are more "bridges." Each individual and every community needs to figure out how to build bridges as a way of participating in the ongoing work of creation and *repristination*—more about that in another chapter—because bridges and transitions are part of life at any age.

If you live long enough, you are going to grow old, at least in chronological years. Aging doesn't progress like some kinds of learning, where you hit a plateau and remain there, willingly or otherwise. And it's not that we expect to ever find the mythical fountain of youth and never grow older. Ponce de Leon went looking for eternal youth and found Florida instead. How's *that* for irony? We know that living forever is neither an option nor an ideal. It's just that it takes some rethinking to accept that the *ultimate* transition, for want of a better word, to a different and *unknown* life will most likely be within the next ten or twenty years.

We all experience transitions, of course, and gaps in-between. For example, when I was a child, it was hard to imagine being a grown-up. No longer being able to make believe or play with toys? What fun could *that* be? As it turns out, however, adulthood *can* be fun. In my early twenties, I couldn't imagine myself as *settled*. In love, yes. I already was. But married and working and becoming a parent? As it turns out, mid-adulthood was and still is one of my favorite times of life. I felt very much part of the real world.

But now comes the question: What will it feel like for me to be a *truly elderly* person, to be on what appears to be the fringes or margins of life?

Transitions, transitions, transitions…from childhood on. Sometimes they were predictably welcome, sometimes unexpectedly so. And sometimes they were considerably more difficult. But all transition involves process—*transition* and *process* being the operative words here. For example, when I quit smoking, it took five tries and roughly fifteen years. (I kept falling for the old, "Can't I have *just one?*") But it has been sixteen years now since I quit for good.

Transition came on a major scale when my husband, Henry, died. I could not imagine how I was going to go on without him, even day to day, let alone for thirty years or more. And yet, little by little, with the grace of God and the help of family and friends, I began to rebuild my life. Do I miss him still? Of course. I do today and will tomorrow and tomorrow and tomorrow. He still is at the heart of my adult life, but I can now enjoy life without him, and I am damn grateful that I can.

I will, of course, have to face more transitions in the years ahead. When I started writing this chapter, I couldn't find the key that I needed until I realized that *transition itself* was the key. At each stage, from childhood on, we can't really anticipate what the next transition will be. We can bring imagination and past experience to bear on the future, but to actually *know* what is going to happen flies in the face of the old saying, "You had to have been there."

Now I'm eighty-one! Good golly, Miss Molly! What now and what next? When I start thinking like this, I have to remember transitions that turned out better than expected and transitions I surely didn't want but worked on and worked out.

18 SHIFTING GEARS
Changes in Speed, Skill, and Perspective

I think I can, I think I can, I think I have a plan.
And I can do 'most anything if I just think I can.
— *The Little Engine That Could*

A lot has been written by healthcare professionals and others about changes in what we can do and can't do as we age...and how well we can or can't do it. A lot of this literature contains valuable information about the changes that may occur and how to cope with them, but as with any "expert" advice, some is less-than-reliable. As our parents and teachers used to tell us, "Consider the source." All sources of information are not equal.

Even when we were young, our particular skills and gifts varied. For example, way back when I was going to night school, I would occasionally serve as a volunteer test subject for psychology graduate students. One of their tests measured adult intelligence. Talk about variations in results! On one part—a vocabulary test—I was practically off the charts. (My children say I know more words than anyone wants to hear.) Another part involved putting little red-and-white patterned blocks together. My husband could do this kind of task lightning fast. Me? I moved them here, I moved them there, I saw no pattern anywhere. Here again, I was practically off the charts—falling right off the bottom! Worse yet were the puzzle pieces, none suggesting anything more to me than a beige blob. Finally, a professor, who walked by the testing booth, said, "For God's sake, Helen, haven't you ever seen an elephant?" The student politely remonstrated that coaching was forbidden. "That's true," the professor said, "but if I didn't, we'd be here all night." He was right. You do not want me to come over and help decide how design your living room.

However, my problem with much of the information on aging is less with the content than with the perspective. That is, many of those who write or speak about aging are some distance in time away from the changes they address. It is one thing to be objective and rational about aging when it is some twenty or thirty or so years away. It's quite another when you're eighty. There is always a fine line between helping and patronizing. You may pat me on the back or shoulder because you like me or I did something good. If you are taller than I, you may even pat me on the head. But you may never patronize me. Well, you may, but you will feel my displeasure. Queen Victoria and I? "We are not amused."

At this point, I am very grateful for the things I can still do. As I said earlier, when I broke my arm, followed by surgery and physical therapy, I learned a lot about the miracle of ordinary life. Being able to do ordinary, everyday things—even so-called homely things like cooking, doing my laundry, and grocery shopping—can be a gift. But there are also things we all need to do differently or shouldn't do at all. Each of us has some specific limitations, challenges, and solutions. Here are some of mine. Maybe they are some of yours.

- **Machines, Muscle, and Me.** I would like to have a bike, but don't. I'm not that confident of my balance and don't want another broken limb. I do a fair amount of walking. Thankfully, I live in a city neighborhood, where many errands are within walking distance. Otherwise, I use public transit or, when necessary, drive. I belong a neighborhood health club and do some simple strengthening exercises there with simple machines. (They have to be simple for me to use them. Mechanics are not my strong point. For example, I won't get on a treadmill for fear I will lose control and be launched into space!)

- **Think or Swim.** Swimming is another prime example of my learning to do things differently. One day when I had access to the health club indoor pool, I jumped in with enthusiasm at the deep end. I hadn't been in a pool much for years and certainly not since I'd broken my arm. I knew swimming could help loosen muscles—repeat, *could*—but only over time. My left arm was so stiff I could only do about three strokes of the crawl, and I was in more than seven feet of water. Being five-foot-four inches tall, I had clearly not made a good decision. Luckily, I was able to backstroke to the side and wade to the steps to haul my injudicious self out of the depths. After that, I started out in the shallow end and gradually increased my range. This is a good rule for retaining and learning skills: *Start shallow and slowly increase the range.*

- **The Knees Have It.** Knees, bless them, can be something of a challenge as we mature. For example, I do some small-scale gardening. We have a small yard with only trees, shrubs, flowers, ground cover, and a little patio in back. (I took out the grass a decade or so ago when I was a mere sixty-something.) Getting down on my knees? I can do it—so there! Getting up again is something else. I have to grab onto a sturdy branch, a trowel, or the hand of a passerby. Once upon a time, I could do a neat genuflection, including a double. Now I figure the Lord is perfectly satisfied with a bow.

- **Words and Music.** I like languages. They give a glimpse of other people, other cultures, and other times. Now and then I still try to learn a new language or go back to one I once studied. I can't memorize words and phrases as I once could, half a century ago, but I am better at recognizing patterns and putting them to use. And I am taking harmonica classes to express whatever song is in my heart. How do you express yours?

- **Driving.** As of this writing, I still drive, and hope to continue to do. I am judicious about times and places. I avoid rush hour in Chicago, if I can, and certain high-traffic, high-speed roads. I will go out of my way to avoid making a left turn at a stoplight, but I always have. I won't attempt to be funny about this topic. Driving is serious business. At any age, we need to recognize our limitations, understand the laws of physics about speed and motion, and apply general common sense. It is also important to recognize that there may come a time when driving is unwise—or worse, dangerous—to others as well as to ourselves. It's a good idea to listen to the opinions of other responsible people about this sensitive topic. It can be very hard to give up the car keys, but it is surely worse to wish you had.

- **Error Message.** I can still make mistakes, even after all these years of learning. My silly swim experience above is only one example. We can certainly expend an undue amount of energy pretending we don't make them, but denial makes it more difficult to correct our mistakes and learn from them. Most of the time, I am able to recognize my errors sooner than later and am willing to acknowledge them. The example of us older folks in this regard can also make younger people feel better about admitting *their* mistakes. Do you really want to spend a lot of time around Pollyanna?

- **And What About You?** What can and do you want to do? What are some of the things you would like to learn, relearn, do, do differently, or maybe even stop doing? Breaking limbs and going prematurely into deep water are bad ideas, but there are other good ones, especially and particularly for *you*.

In case you would like a few more suggestions for growing old gracefully, here they are. They are included in the price of the book. If not, ignore them.

- **Exercise.** You know the old saying: "Use it or lose it." Not everyone wants to or can join a health club or Y, but we can do simple exercises at home. For example, I have low-weight hand weights I use. Take my advice: If you use weights or do intense exercise, do so on alternate days to give your muscles time to rest. And inform yourself about how to exercise. Take a class, consult a trainer, or a read a good book. Be judicious. Don't be a fool like I was in that pool.

- **Exercise the Mind.** Again, use it or lose it. Give your brain some exercise. Give it some fun. Learn something new, or relearn something old. The world around us is waiting to be discovered. Whenever possible, find someone to share your interests, preferably in person but, if not, in cyberspace. (The internet is a great place for us seniors in this regard, but we have to use it with some caution. Not everyone out there is as sane, sweet, and sensible as we are.)

- **Exercise the Spirit.** What acts of prayer, service, worship, community, make room for the Spirit in your life?

- **Read.** Get a good book about growing older. I personally like the works of Dr. Andrew Weil, but there are many other good ones. Avoid books that patronize, insult, or age you prematurely!

- **Add Color.** Bring *your* gifts. The great Italian painter Titian was still painting in his nineties, even though he probably reached his peak when he was a mere youngster in his seventies. There are many other examples, including mystery writer P.D. James, politician Jimmy Carter, and musicians Leonard Cohen, Aretha Franklin, and Mick Jagger.

- **Remember.** A classic Rolls or a Mercedes is still a Rolls or a Mercedes even when traveling at reduced speed. And we who are "up in age" are all, of course, *classics.*

19 YOU GOTTA HAVE A DREAM....
Reimagining the Future

Happy talk, keep talking happy talk, Talk about things you like to do. You gotta have a dream, If you don't have a dream, how you gonna have a dream come true?

— *South Pacific*

South Pacific first appeared on Broadway in 1949, four years after the end of World War II, and was made into a film in 1958 and again in 2001. "Happy Talk," quoted above, is sung by Bloody Mary, a wise Polynesian woman who has experienced the challenges of holding onto dreams in real life. More than sixty years after she first sang these words, they still ring true.

Dreams can be for ourselves, for others, for one and all. Dr. Martin Luther King's "I Have a Dream" speech still echoes in minds and hearts decades after his violent death at the age of thirty-nine. No, his dream hasn't been fully realized. Racism and other forms of prejudice still exist. But his dream has become more of a reality precisely because of the work of men and women he inspired.

Dreams have always been a part of literature, music, and life. We read of dreams in both the Hebrew Scriptures and the New Testament. Joseph, the son of Jacob, interprets the dreams of Egypt's Pharaoh. Joseph, betrothed of Mary, is told in a dream to go ahead and marry her. Later, after the birth of Jesus, he is warned in a dream to leave for Egypt to escape his son's death at the hands of Herod's troops. In the Book of Acts, we read that Peter changed his views on what constitutes clean and unclean through a dream.

There are dreams we dream when we're asleep, and those we dream when we're awake. They can be wonderful, confusing, or scary. Our dreams may stay the same, but they can and often do change over time. Life would be much less interesting and much less hopeful without them. Think back on some of your own past dreams. Think of your dreams now. We all dream of happy and productive lives for our children and those we love, and we dream that for ourselves as well. Sometimes we elders think—or can be made to feel—that dreams are only for the young. Well, they certainly *are* for the young, but they are not *only* for the young.

When I was young, I mean *really* young, I had my own dreams. First, I wanted to be a cowboy—with a horse, of course. As I got a little older, about ten or twelve, I got more realistic. Instead, I wanted to become a writer—preferably a famous novelist, marry a rancher, and live in Montana—with the horse, of course. I also dreamed of traveling in general and especially to Europe. At that time, going to either coast would have been wildly adventurous for me, and Europe seemed an impossible dream. You either had to be rich or serving in the military to see the world back then. But the travel dream persisted—literally. I once had a wonderful, vivid, black-and-white dream of being in England. The black-and-white part was a beautiful, unidentified marble floor. I thought to myself, "Wow! I actually made it!" And then I woke up.

I didn't marry a rancher and live in Montana. I married a psychologist, had three children, and lived in Chicago. And I am glad of it. Bless you, Henry J. Lambin—even though I never did get that horse.

I did eventually write, off and on, but not until considerably later. First, when I was working and going to college, the only things I wrote were term papers, and I did not like writing term papers! I especially did not like doing them on a manual typewriter. Anyone remember those? All that retyping when you made mistakes or revisions? It wasn't until after I married and had children that I returned to writing, and it wasn't until some years later that I think I actually *became* a writer. That's when I turned to writing as a way of dealing with loss and transition. I simply had to write. And now most of it, thank God, has been on computer! I never did become rich and famous, but, yes, I became a writer because, as a long-ago writer friend of my husband said, "What do writers do? Writers write."

As far as travel? I have done some in the United States and even in Europe, although not as much as I'd have liked to have done or for nearly as long. (As my mother used to say, "Now if I were rich, instead of so good-looking....") Some thirty years after the dream of the black-and-white marble floor, I actually did see it in person at London's St. Paul's Cathedral. I was every bit as excited and ecstatic as I had been in that long-ago dream.

Sometimes dreams take some adjusting, temporarily or more permanently. For example, I dreamed of living somewhere other than Chicago for a change—someplace *different*—on a river near LaCrosse, Wisconsin, or in exotic (to me) Montreal. I'm still here in Chicago, but I'm also surely grateful to be in my own home.

I also dreamed of retiring and having more time to spend with Henry, that he would live to be at least eighty, a healthy eighty, for his sake and mine. I did eventually retire, and enjoy it, but Henry died at age seventy-four, and I have been a widow now for nineteen years. Yes, I can enjoy life and am grateful for these days, but still, I dream that one day (not too soon, though) I will see Henry's smile of welcome once again—that is, if I shape up and improve my general character!

When my arm was in the immobilizer, my big dream was simply to be as I was before the break—what I termed *normal.* After the surgery, however, when I was able to return to church, cordial congregants raised eyebrows when I said *normal.* The implication was that I was trying to return to a state I had never occupied in the first place. I think they were probably right.

What does it take for our dreams to come true? Work, working together, vision, thought, prayer, reflection, unselfishness, generosity, scientific discoveries, what some might call miracles, timing, planning, and what my father used to call, in relation to card games, "damn fool luck." Since I can't do much about "damn fool luck," I will devote the next chapter, more or less, to planning.

20 GARBAGE ROUGHS
Respecting and Restructuring Plans

Make no little plans; they have no magic to stir men's blood
and probably themselves will not be realized. Make big plans;
aim high in hope and work, remembering that a noble, logical
diagram once recorded will not die.
— Daniel Hudson Burnham

The quote above is from a world famous city planner. Okay, maybe we
need to carefully define, or restrict, the meaning of *little* in his philoso-
phy. But Burnham had it right when he advised thinking big, aiming
high. He made room for yesterdays, and he looked ahead to tomorrows.
He dreamed, planned, and began work on his plans in his *today*. That
goes for our today as well. We need to make plans, make room for hope
and the kind of magic—or miracle—that stirs our blood. We need to do
some planning for tomorrow.

Remember, everything doesn't have to be worked out perfectly today. Plans don't have to be set in stone. Sometimes, maybe many times,
they need to be restructured. This becomes more apparent as we grow a
little older, but the truth is, young or old or anywhere along the contin-
uum, we all have to restructure our plans repeatedly. Much, if not all, of
this chapter could be devoted to quotes confirming that, but I'll restrain
myself and share only a few.

- "The best laid schemes o' mice and men Gang aft a-gley
  [don't work out]." Robert Burns

- "If you want to make God laugh, tell Him your plans."
  Woody Allen

- "Life is what happens to us while we're making other plans." Alan Saunders (Yes, John Lennon had a nice song about this, but Saunders said it first in the January 1957 edition of *Reader's Digest*.)

- "Always, well, usually, well, sometimes anyway, have Plans B, C, and D. And leave room for promptings of the Spirit." Helen Lambin

The advice above does not mean—repeat, does *not* mean—that we need not plan in the first place. If, as the song from *South Pacific* goes, "you gotta have a dream," you've also usually got to have a plan—albeit a plan with some flexibility, some room to grow and change. This is where the "garbage rough" metaphor comes in.

When I begin working on a writing project, sometimes it goes smoothly almost immediately and the words come skipping and slipping in. Other times it does not come at all smoothly or quickly or easily. I really have to struggle with it. That is when I use what I call a garbage rough, a rough draft. It's not that I consider it garbage in the sense of being worthless or not worth caring about. I do care about it, a lot, or I wouldn't be writing about it. It's more in the idea that I know I can use some parts of the draft, discard others, combine them differently, or change them radically. The key point being that, at this point in the process, the garbage rough does not have to be *good*. The idea is to get something down on paper—or in the computer. A garbage rough is much less intimidating than a blank sheet of paper or a blank screen. Believe me.

I did it—inadvertently—with this chapter. I thought I had completed it, but I awoke in the middle of the night to decide that I had not. It wasn't right at all or, rather, it was only partially okay. So I thought about it and debated it and finally figured it out to my satisfaction—yes, still in the middle of the night. And central to my success was, ironically—what else?—the garbage rough.

There is certainly such a thing as over-planning. We all need room for some spontaneity in life. But wise planning and prudent action can give shape to our lives and become an balanced approach to realizing our dreams. Yes, even the best laid schemes do "Gang aft a-gley." That's when you consider plans B, C, and so on, or maybe just listen to the promptings of the Spirit for Plan E or even Z.

If you have had as many birthdays as I have, where does that leave planning and dreaming? You probably know the stock questions prospective employers and self-improvement articles ask: "What do you want to be in five or ten years?" At one time I would have had to stop and think about those questions. Now my first response is simply, "Preferably alive and well."

I could probably note (needlessly) that I don't know how many years I have left. Actually, when it comes right down to it, most of us don't. But when you are eighty, it is unlikely to be many years. Can I still have dreams? Can I still make plans? Well, actually, I *have* to, because that's me.

For example, I am a great one for making New Year's resolutions. I have been making them almost every year for decades—often recycling the same ones. I am also one for breaking things into what I consider manageable chunks, setting small goals leading toward larger goals. For example, I don't plan to lose ten or twenty pounds. I plan to lose five. And then another five. (Actually, I haven't lost that first five yet, but you get the idea.) I have always had things I wanted and needed to do, learn, change, improve—including improving me.

At the present time my self-improvement agenda includes (but is not restricted to) relearning some Spanish, keeping in better touch with friends, volunteering, improving my character, exercise, learning the harmonica, improving my character, better nutrition, losing a few pounds, spiritual growth, improving my character, learning a little about the mysteries of the universe (or universes?) and, finally, travel—whatever I can manage in time, energy, and money—destination presently unknown.

So I'm going to keep planning, damn it, for whatever time I have left. I hope that time isn't too short, what with my being twenty-four going on eighty-one. Some may technically be "little" plans—sorry, Daniel Burnham—but they will still be plans and dreams.

21 HERE I (UNEXPECTEDLY) STAND
Pathway to Pilgrimage

> Free to good church.
> Has all shots.
> — Rosemary Lambin

My daughter Rosemary offered to post the words above along with my photo in various churches to help me along with my pilgrimage—the pilgrimage I didn't even know I was making.

When I decided to take a sabbatical from my Roman Catholic parish in September of 2004, I did not know that within a year I would have become a liberal Lutheran and then a member of the Episcopal church in my neighborhood. And I could never have imagined that I would be threatened with formal excommunication by the Roman Catholic Archbishop of Chicago.

Even now, roughly nine years after I began that "sabbatical," I am still at times in a state of disbelief at the way things turned out. I'll stop in the middle of whatever I am doing and think: "What have I done? How did I get to this place?" My disbelief is not from a sense of feeling guilty. If I had felt guilty about leaving my previous church, I would have stayed. Rather, my disbelief is from a sense of complete surprise and, when I think about it, gratitude. (It has occurred to me off and on as I grow older that, while planning and preparing is certainly essential, I have drifted into a lot of the good things in life as if carried along by an unseen stream.)

Back to the beginning of my pilgrimage. In September of 2004, I decided I needed to explore other spiritual options. At least that is the way I put it to myself. Whatever I was doing wasn't working. I was going through the motions as if some grown-up was telling what to do, except that in this case I was the alleged grown-up.

In looking back, some of this undoubtedly grew out of the sudden death of my husband in 1996. Overnight my world had changed in every way, including my relationship to my parish and the Catholic Church. All those years, all those Sundays, we had gone to Mass—first as a family, then as a couple. It had been a comfortable, comforting routine. Then it was gone. At the same time, faith in some form kept me alive, kept me going through the worst of times. Faith—or hope—that death was not the end of love.

But more immediately, I had increasing difficulties with the Roman Catholic Church's positions on various social issues: divorce and remarriage, contraception, and attitudes toward gays and lesbians to name a few. I did not think these policies served the prophetic voice of faith. My views were ironic for a straight, gray-haired, widowed granny, I suppose, but what if *my* child, for example, was gay? Because every gay child, every lesbian, every divorced and remarried Catholic is always *someone's* child.

Whatever the reasons leading up to my decision, I realized I was almost fresh out of faith and that, if I was ever to find God, I was going to have to go looking for him or her elsewhere. What I suspect now is that more likely God was already looking for *me*. At that point I felt awkward dignifying my quest with the word *pilgrimage*, but I can't think of any other word for it. It's a time-honored word for all kinds of journeys.

But still, to even think of leaving the Catholic Church? Many of my Catholic friends share my concerns, but they remain faithful to their religion in the best sense. When I began my pilgrimage, I imagined I would wind up back where I was—in a Catholic parish. I couldn't imagine being anything else. I had no trouble with other people following their paths in other faith traditions. That was fine, and I could talk with and learn from them. But for a life-long Catholic? I thought things were different for me. It seemed simple and self-evident: I may have been a Practicing Catholic, a Cafeteria Catholic, or Fallen-Away Catholic, but I was not *Something Else.*

I had been a practicing Catholic for more than sixty years, from my childhood into my life in Chicago, where I graduated from and ultimately worked for a Catholic university. It was in Chicago that I met Henry J. Lambin, psychologist, loving father and husband, and life-long Catholic. Over the years I was active in Catholic parish life. But somehow, through the grace of God, I wound up following a different faith path.

But back to my leaving—or being asked to leave—the Catholic Church. What happened was this. Sometime in late winter 2004, I wrote a letter to the Cardinal Archbishop of Chicago, suggesting that the bishops were out of touch with ordinary people. As a result, I was later invited to become a part of the Archdiocesan Pastoral Council, a kind of advisory council for the Cardinal. This was a generous invitation and response. Each member of the Archdiocesan Pastoral Council served on a committee, and I asked for and was appointed to the Social Justice Committee. And that was the beginning of what would become the end.

The end began when I questioned how the prophetic voice of the Church was and should be raised, particularly on behalf of divorced and remarried Catholics and our gay and lesbian brothers and sisters. Eventually I concluded that I could no longer represent a "traditional" Catholic population. Out of respect for the Cardinal and his position, I wrote a letter of resignation to him, stating why I was resigning to pursue other Christian spiritual paths. So began my pilgrimage.

Here is an excerpt from my letter.

My reasons are both personal and on principle. Regarding the latter: When the Church addresses social justice issues, like minimum wage, affordable housing, accessible health care, peace among nations, and prejudice, this is the Church that speaks with a prophetic voice. But there are other issues, I think, that do not reflect this prophetic voice.

Among these are the following. The Church seeks to end abortions, yet opposes birth control. It will not allow divorced Catholics to remarry, yet will grant annulments when a marriage has existed for years, and with children. It does not accept long-term committed relationships among lesbians and homosexuals, yet affirms the sanctity of marriage.... I am a straight, gray-haired granny...[who] was lucky enough to have a wonderful husband.... But the gays and lesbians, these are also my brothers and sisters, some surely more spiritual and selfless than I. And had I been less lucky in my marriage, the divorced woman in the pew could have been me.

Because of the LGBT concerns in the letter, I sent a copy to Joe Murray, the head of the Chicago Rainbow Sash Movement. I received a form letter—a postcard—of acknowledgment from an assistant to the Cardinal, but nothing else. Nothing, that is, until Joe Murray asked to circulate my letter on the Rainbow Sash website. He explained that there is a high suicide rate among young gay men and felt that my letter would represent a kind of affirmation from the mainstream. I said yes. I also sent a second letter to the Cardinal, informing him how and why the letter would be circulated. I didn't want him be taken by surprise. Now things suddenly became, shall we say, lively.

First, I received a request from an assistant to the Cardinal, asking for a copy of the first letter, which had either gone missing or was possibly in the Cardinal's mailbag on the way to Rome. I did. The Cardinal, I was told, would respond on his return from a trip to Rome. He did. The response was a letter from the Cardinal, enclosing a copy of a typewritten form called "REQUEST TO LEAVE THE CATHOLIC CHURCH BY A FORMAL ACT." It would appear that the form hadn't been used in some time—a *long* time—since the typeface indicated it was done on a typewriter and then photocopied. According to the instructions, the form was to be signed and notarized and then returned to the Office of the Chancellor.

I think the form was misnamed. This was not a request. It was a kind of "DO-IT-YOURSELF EXCOMMUNICATION" form, sternly warning me I could no longer receive the sacraments in the Catholic Church. I have always had respect for the sacraments. To agree not to receive them again would have been wholly dishonest on my part. From my perspective, it is the Table of the Lord, open to all, not one with a card proclaiming "Reserved for Members Only." The form also warned me that I could not have Catholic burial rites. My husband is buried in St. Boniface Cemetery in the Lambin family plot, and someday I intend to be buried beside him. And yes, there is room for me in the family plot, Protestant or not. I know, I checked. The dead are sometimes more open-minded that the living.

What would you do? I didn't sign the form the Cardinal had sent. Eventually, I returned it unsigned, saying I would not, could not, should not, sign it because I intend to be buried with my husband in a Catholic cemetery. I doubt that the authorities would oppose that. I *could not* sign it because I was still planning to remain a Christian—Catholic or otherwise—the work of a lifetime. And said I *should not* sign it, because it should never have been sent to me or to anyone else.

I did, however, continue my pilgrimage. In April of 2005, I joined Immanuel Evangelical Lutheran Church in Chicago and remained there until autumn of 2014. (Yes, I let them know my story. They knew what they were getting.) Do I miss being Catholic, after being part of the Church for so many years? Yes. There were many things I loved about Catholic spirituality and culture. I am Catholic acculturated. And breaking up is hard to do. Did my faith community at Immanuel have meaning for me in terms of worship, spirituality, social justice, and community? Yes, it did. And it is where I began to recognize the presence in my life of that Gracious God. So I am grateful. But I am still learning. Once a pilgrim....

When I joined Immanuel, Rev. Robert Goldstein was the pastor. With insight that wasn't so evident to me at the time, he said, "This may not be the end of your pilgrimage." I couldn't imagine what he meant. Wasn't enough enough? Well, not quite. Pastor Goldstein, now retired, evidently had it right.

As I write this chapter, I have become a member of the Church of the Atonement, the Episcopal church in my neighborhood. I only recently began attending liturgy there, but was drawn to it. One obvious attraction was that the theology and ritual of the Episcopal Church as I experience it at Atonement have much in common with what I so valued in the Catholic Church. Another factor is that, in some ways, I feel more at home there, even as a newcomer, which is always a challenge for me. Even so, this was a difficult decision. I learned a lot at Immanuel

Lutheran. I met people I like very much and respect for their commitment to the good of their church and the community, for their skill and grace in carrying it their mission. But having spent more than sixty years of my life as a Roman Catholic, there is much I still miss, even now. Atonement seems like a better fit. Perhaps I am growing just a bit old for all this pilgrim's progress.

Still, once a pilgrim....

So ironically enough, at the age of seventy-two in the year 2005, I wound up saying, in effect, what a thirty-something reformist Augustinian monk (Martin Luther) had said nearly 500 years before in his response to Rome: "Here I stand; I can do no other."

Were I to write my original letter to the Cardinal now, I would undoubtedly also include something about the second-class status of women in the Church. When I left I was uncomfortable with the way the Church treated women, but it was not yet a foundational issue for me. After all, it was what I was used to. I have done a lot of thinking over the last nine years and have come to feel more and more strongly about all of these issues of justice and full inclusion for all God's children. As long as women cannot fully participate in ministry as priests and as bishops, and as long as they have no real voice in decision-making, they will remain second-class—make that third-class—citizens in the Kingdom of God. The Catholic Church will be deprived of the gifts and vision of half its population and remain the poorer for it. Having women in ordained ministry would bring new gifts, new vision, and a broader horizon. The question is not: "How can we possibly *have* women priests and bishops?" The real question is: "How can we possibly *not have* women bishops and priests?"

The Episcopalians dealt with that issue for many years, and it was painful process for them, but they came out on the right side of it, and so, I pray, will the Catholics. But for me, I have found a new spiritual home, one where I am more in harmony with the approach to issues like who can be called to the priesthood and who can fall in love.

Some 2,000 years ago a woman became the mother of God through the power of the Holy Spirit. Surely then, through the continuing power of the Spirit, women are qualified to be priests. "Holy Mary, mother of God...." we pray. Should we not begin to live it?

22 NOW, WHERE DID I PUT IT?
Lost and Found by Faith

Faith doesn't get you around problems in life and relationships, it gets you through it.
— Jonathan Anthony Burkett

I lose things. Or I place them properly but forget where. And, no, it's not what people call, pseudo-humorously, a "senior moment." (I refuse to dignify that phrase with caps.) I have been losing things for as long as I can remember—not always, but too often. The list of the lost includes tote bags, books, scarves, gloves, caps, keys, glasses, pens, money, and rosaries. The rosaries were casualties of travel. One, for example, went missing on a boat from Sweden to Finland. The replacement rosary, which I still have, triggered alarms and a pat-down at O'Hare Airport in Chicago when I forgot to take it out of my pocket. Maybe God was trying to tell me something—if nothing else, maybe to actually use it instead of just bringing it along when I leave town.

The New Orleans rosary loss was the most troubling. It was plain, black, decades old. And it had belonged to my mother, now deceased. Reared Presbyterian, she converted to Catholicism as a young adult, although not through marriage. (My father was a P.K.—preacher's kid.) Even after she returned to the Presbyterian Church in her seventies, my mother continued to say the rosary. And before that, my father, the P.K., hospitalized with a heart attack, had said it for people he heard moaning in the night. It's not for nothing that the rosary, with its reflection and repetition, has been called the great Catholic mantra. I really regretted losing that irreplaceable set of beads.

When my children were young, they heard a common refrain delivered with a plaintive whine (mine): "Help me find...." My son Joe suggested using string to attach everything I own directly to me. It might have been a good idea for things physical. I don't suppose it would have helped much with my loss of faith. Yes, periodically I have lost that too—left it behind in a hurry.

When you come right down to it, having faith takes faith. And having faith becomes, at least for me, more accessible with a Loving and Lovable God, rather than a God to be Feared. Mine is the God celebrated by some of the psalmists and prophets, the God who could say: "I've called your name, you're mine" (Isaiah 43:1).

The God I first believed in was quite different. He was "keeping tabs." And he—no possibility of using *she* then—was a really strict CPA (Critical Private Accountant) who couldn't wait to balance the books. Attempted personal reform or not, I was a card-carrying member of the Hyper-Sinners Brigade. Grace—call it sanctifying or just plain grace—was and is a grand thing, but unfortunately I was quite sure that my grace account was seriously overdrawn. What I definitely needed was a more flexible, more understanding, more *lavish* God, one who dispensed grace to the needy, not just to the deserving and the greedy. This is the God of some of the nicest "ordinary" people, and it is the God of the late, great Saint John XXIII, who manifested this presence in his papacy and person.

There are, of course, countless hints of this Loving God's presence in our everyday lives. We hear and see it in the words and actions of other people—and other creatures. It comes in an up-springing of joy for no apparent reason other than the advent of a lovely summer or fall day. And it comes in the beauty of a spring shower or a starry winter sky. God's presence can also be noticed at some of the worst times in our lives, when faith can be hardest to hold on to and yet is most sorely needed to help us get through the days to come and even the moment at hand.

Faith can seem to disappear for any number of reasons—problems, preoccupations, things going really badly, or even things going distractingly well. And sometimes, too many times probably, at least in my case, it disappears from carelessness. "Now where did I put it…?"

But whether from carelessness or other reasons, losing my faith *matters*. I am supposed to be practicing Christianity, but I don't practice hard enough or do it sloppily or inattentively. For me, however, a world without faith would be like a world with too little oxygen or one lived in too narrow a room with low ceilings and no windows.

Generally speaking, I can live with occasionally losing things—except for that old black rosary. Surely we can all name our more painful losses: loved ones, pets, homes, love, comfort, security, hope. But for me, faith is a biggie. Wherever it is—misplaced, lost, or strayed (not stolen), I *need* it. Although I consider myself a Christian, I am far from actually being a good one. On the other hand, consider how much worse a person I would be if I weren't!

I'm not making a universal statement about the need for the Christian faith. I know highly-principled people, some of my favorite people among them, who are of other faiths or are not part of my religious community. Nor do I go along with the us-vs.-them-space-and-place argument about heaven, a theology which holds that only those who share my belief system are given admission tickets.

So I'm not in the spirituality game for the prizes, but I need all the help I can get, especially the help that comes from being part of a faith community. It's not that I think of going to church and being part of a faith community as some kind of After-Life Insurance. God's grace is for everyone. Otherwise, Loving God wouldn't be Loving God. But I draw life and hope from worship, word, and sacrament, and from being part of a faith community that shares, supports, and serves.

I don't—I can't—deny the existence of sin. Who, witnessing utter cruelty and selfishness and self-serving indifference close up or from a distance, can deny there is evil in the world? And yes, I think we are all going to be held accountable for our actions—sometime, somewhere, and somehow. God is justice and mercy both. I'm not God, so I don't have to worry about it, obviously, but I am a mother and a grandmother. What parent could wish and order that his or her child suffer forever? Instead, we want them to learn and grow, to be responsible and giving, to be happy and make others so.

As I said, I'm not God (does that need repeating?), but I envision purgatory as something like the ultimate learning experience, including tough love when necessary for the worst offenders. In my idea of purgatory, we each watch re-runs of our lives—what we did, what we failed to do, and how our action or inaction affected others. Eventually, sooner or later—or much, much, much later—we look at the hurt we or have caused, in whole or in part, and cry out in shame and even horror at what we have done. We react whole-heartedly with genuine sorrow, "If only I could do that over again, I would do it so much differently!"

Then we are ready to move on, finally prepared to enjoy heaven—like any well-prepared person reaching his or her destination after a long journey.

Oh, and one more thing. Remember that old black rosary of my mother's I felt so bad about losing? After nearly four years, my daughter

Rosemary found it while searching for something at the back of a closet. There it was in its little coin purse in a box of forgotten hair bows and barrettes. Don't ask me how it got there or even how she happened to find it. I only know how delighted I was and still am! I was convinced that I would never see it again. It was gone forever. And then it was not.

This is a prayer I found in my notes. I wrote it some time ago and put it away for later use, expecting it might have meaning for me in the future. And it does.

Why is it, Lord, that we didn't find each other before? Why didn't you look harder for me? Why didn't I let myself be found? I really could have been a better person, Lord, to all around me. I think of what and who and how I could have been, and all the things I would have, could have, and especially should have done differently, better, or not at all. So, is it too late, Eternal God? I guess in your view there's always a second, or a third, or a hundred and thirty-ninth chance. So maybe I should just give up griping and give myself over to you.

A dialogue between Jesus and some annoyed and perplexed Pharisees triggered this story: "Suppose one of you had a hundred sheep and lost one. Wouldn't you leave the ninety-nine in the wilderness and go after the lost one until you found it? When found, you can be sure you would put it across your shoulders, rejoicing, and when you got home call in your friends and neighbors saying 'Celebrate with me! I've found my lost sheep!' Count on it—there's more joy in heaven over one sinner's rescued life than over ninety-nine good people in no need of rescue" (Luke 15:3-7).

I said in the previous chapter that I am glad now that I went on my spiritual pilgrimage, and I acknowledged that I am very likely still on one. I think that part of faith is losing it and finding it again—or rather, being found by it. Sometimes, in some ways, I think maybe faith is like my lost rosary. When you least expect it, you find it again. Unexpectedgrace is the best kind.

23 LUUUV CALLS AND ISLANDS RISING
Voices and Vision

Bali Ha'i will whisper
On the wind of the sea:
"Here am I, Your special island!
Come to me, come to me!"
— *South Pacific*

I'm going to mix metaphors here. The metaphors are *luuuv calls* and *mysterious islands*. I hope you'll bear with me as I try to tie them together.

Now for the first metaphor. Some twenty years back, when my daughter Jeanne was nineteen or twenty or so, I would answer the phone to hear, "This is a luuuv call." That introduction meant we were going to talk about dating. And relationships. And about luuuuuv. And that's the main theme of this chapter. Luuuv.

I don't do well with pure abstraction, including the Being we call God. It's not that I expect some kind of definition or description. I can't define God, I can't begin to comprehend God, and I don't expect to. (I don't even understand my computer!) But what I do know is this: I don't need or want a personal relationship with my computer, but I *do* need and want a personal relationship with God. God and me. Me and God. Not that I've succeeded in that relationship. I'm just saying it's something I seek. You can call it love. A luuuv call.

Some experts are uncomfortable with what some Christians describe as a "personal relationship" with God or with Jesus. They are afraid it will lead to some kind of exclusive relationship. God and Me. *Period.* They have a point. A "personal relationship" can become exclusive and isolating, but it doesn't have to and it isn't meant to.

So here's a topic I'd like to examine…with the usual disclaimer that I'm not a theologian, psychologist, or sociologist. I'm not even an expert on love or romance. I suppose, technically, you could say my last date was more than fifty years ago. But I *can* distinguish between two very basic types or phases of an important relationship, whether it's romantic, friendship, parental, whatever. So let's talk about luuuv.

First there is the You-and-Me phase. And that's it. You and me. A small circle. No room for anyone else. A relationship may start out that way, but it can't stay that way. If it does, it ceases to be love and becomes possession. At best, it is selfish. At worse, it is dangerous. Think stalkers, for example.

Then there is the other kind of relationship, the kind in which loving and being loved moves beyond boundaries and becomes more inclusive and generous. Being loved and loving someone else brings with it the impulse to invite others into that circle. Think of the times you felt happiest and most a part of things. Did you look inward or outward? I believe genuine love will always move outward, will always be inclusive. Just as this is true of human relationships, I think it is in our relationship with God.

Look at the some of the stories and lessons in the Scriptures. Remember that quotation from Isaiah and his wonderful voice of God? "Don't be afraid, I've redeemed you. I've called your name. You're mine" (Isaiah 43:1). And who is that *you*? Is it you personally or is it "y'all," as they say in Georgia? Yes, it is you *and* God. "You personally are mine. You personally I have called by name." Yes, it applies to a people—*all people*—but not an anonymous blob. It's you and you and you and you and me and everyone who reads this and everyone who doesn't: "I have called *y'all* by name."

I've said this elsewhere, and I'll say it again. I have three children—Joe, Rosemary, and Jeanne. Joe is my favorite. So is Rosemary. So is Jeanne. Each of them. Don't ask me to explain it. It's just the way it is. And I think that is the way it is with God. Each of us is God's favorite. Don't ask me to explain it. It's just the way it is.

In December of 2011, I was in Sweden and Finland. I was captivated by all the islands off much of the Baltic Sea coast, especially near Finland, islands which form an archipelago or archipelagos. The islands emerge from land that has been pressed down, weighed down, during a previous ice age, by the sheer weight of the ice. And then, little by little, over centuries, over millennia, the land begins to rise up out of the Baltic Sea to form necklaces of inhabitable and life-giving islands. Even with brooding gray skies, leaden sea, and seasonal darkness, it was beautiful, mesmerizing, and breathtaking.

Thinking about it, I discovered a metaphor for the presence of God in our lives. That is, we are weighed down by our own ice age, our own limitations, by human strengths and frailties, by pressures and sorrows and failings and losses. Sometimes the weight and the coldness and darkness seem more than we can bear. But there is hope. There is faith. And there is love. The luuuv call.

God's love for us, expressed best for Christians in Jesus of Nazareth, helps to melt the ice of our burdens and limitations. It enables us to rise, like those islands, emerging little by little from our hidden darkness, with love and mystery. Like those mysterious islands, together we form a necklace, one that reaches around and around the world. And like them, embraced by God's love—individually and together, we become beautiful and alive and life-giving. A call-and-response luuuv call.

24 SITTING WITH GOD
A Listening, Speaking Heart

One day he was praying in a certain place. When he finished, one of his disciples said, "Master, teach us to pray just as John taught his disciples."

— Luke 11:1

As I approach the end of this book, I realize I haven't covered a significant topic, one that is often missing in my daily, weekly, and even yearly life as well. And that topic is prayer.

Prayer can be an ecstatic response in times of joy. It can be an essential response in times of great difficulty. It can be life giving and life sustaining. That being said, I don't do it nearly as often or in nearly as focused a way as I should. Almost every year for decades I have made a New Year's resolution to pray more, and, ultimately, for decades I haven't followed through. To borrow a phrase from T. S. Elliott, I start out each year with a bang and end with a whimper. Nevertheless, I'll keep on making that resolution, because it is well worth it. Only maybe I should consider making it only on a month-to-month—or day-to-day—basis.

Public prayer, private prayer, prayers of thanksgiving, intercessory prayer, learned and memorized prayer, prayer of silence, centering prayer, and still more. There are so many different *kinds* of prayer and so many different *approaches* to prayer. Each has merit, and no one size fits all— not all persons, not all occasions. So, what are some of the ways in which they differ? How can they help in times of transition? And, the more basic question, what exactly is prayer?

I recall the definition in the *Baltimore Catechism*, once memorized by generations of Catholics. According to the catechism, prayer was the lifting up of the mind and heart to God. That still seems a good definition, but it depends on how you define *lifting up*. It also has the potential to make God seem somewhere up there, out there, and above all—in one word—distant.

I define prayer as presence and conversation. Try to sit with God as if you were sitting in a room with an old, cherished friend. Maybe sitting in silence, maybe talking. As you would in all true conversation, you also try to listen attentively and respond appropriately.

Neat idea, isn't it? But actually doing it is not so easy. I start reasonably focused, with good intentions, breathing deeply, growing calm, and trying to put myself in the picture—sort of putting God and myself together—if you can picture God in some kind of chair in some kind of room. And then, before I know it, my mind has gone off on its own. Not only has that train left the station, but my mind has apparently left the room. It is easy to get distracted.

One of the things you *don't* want to do in this kind of prayer is to try to fight those distractions. Fighting them just makes them stronger. One suggestion I learned in a meditation group is to put the distractions on a log in a swift-flowing river and just let them float away. If you need them back, you can always retrieve them later. The meditation group was one of the forms of prayer and meditation I experienced over the years. I'll give a few examples of types, methods, and settings I continue to draw from.

The Women's Meditation Group

This experience was led by Sister Fran Glowsinki, OSF, then a member of the Loyola University of Chicago ministry team. Other groups, at other times, were offered for students in general, men and women both.

Ours was an opportunity for women employees of the university to come together once a week over our lunch hour. When Sister Fran became a hospital chaplain, our group came to an end, but much of what I learned and experienced then, some fifteen to twenty years ago, remains with me still.

Sister Fran used a form of *guided meditation*. It began with members sitting quietly and comfortably, breathing deeply and slowly. Then we were led through a meditation exercise with lots of room for silence. There are a variety of these kinds of exercises, many described in detail in books. One of my favorites was this. (It's been a while, so I hope I have it right, dear Fran.)

Picture yourself walking down a path somewhere, taking in the place, the season, the sounds, and the feeling. Eventually you wind up at the door of a house. (Take the time to see the house, but avoid getting lost in furnishing it, as a work colleague and I sometimes did.) Enter the house, experiencing its quiet, comfort, warmth, welcome, and a kind of meaning special to you. Someone else may or may not be present, but whomever you encounter will always be a *benign* someone. Remain in peace and calm for a while. When you leave to return to everyday world, you know you can always return to this place when you so choose.

The Lord's Prayer

I have said the Lord's Prayer for more than sixty years, but apparently I wasn't paying close attention, particularly to the beginning: "Our Father." Those are the exact words Jesus taught. One day when I said them, I suddenly stopped dead in my tracks—metaphorically, not literally. (One of my pet peeves is people using *literally* when they mean *metaphorically*. Okay, you're forgiven.)

When I experienced the insight—or revelation, if you will, I was praying a somewhat different translation of the passage in Matthew's Gospel. (See Matthew 6:9-15.) This one was in *The New Revised Standard Version*. Different people and different communities prefer different versions of the prayer, some the more traditional one, some the newer one. This one begins simply "Our Father in heaven" instead of "Our Father who art in heaven." There is no relative clause—no Who or Which. And that is literally as far as I got for quite some time. It was, in a sense, like saying "my mother or father in Iowa." It seemed so definite, so real, and so clear. There was, for a moment, the profound sense of a Real Person Somewhere—but a Person far beyond anything or anyone I could imagine. And this was the Person I was talking to! The experience lasted only for a moment, of course, before distractions came unbidden, but I know now that it is *there*. And sometimes I can be too.

Centering Prayer

For a definition of this form of prayer, I'll turn to Wikipedia since it offers a concise definition and brief history. The entry reads: "Centering prayer is a popular method of contemplative prayer or Christian meditation, placing emphasis on interior silence." It has roots in early Christian monastic practices like those of the desert fathers and mothers and the Benedictines. It can be found in the works of writers like St. Teresa of Avila, St. John of the Cross, and the anonymous author of the wonderfully titled *The Cloud of Unknowing*. Its resurgence in Catholic communities and those of other denominations owes a big debt to the work of Father William Meninger, Father M. Basil Pennington, and Abbot Thomas Keating, all Trappist monks of St. Joseph's Abbey in Spencer, Massachusetts.

At present I participate in a Centering Prayer group at Immanuel Lutheran Church the third Saturday morning of each month. It was founded by Stan Wood, a gifted layman from Church of the Atonement. Centering prayer is *ecumenical*. Sometimes I debate about dragging my busy self or my lazy self out on a Saturday morning. Each time I'm glad I did. I come away feeling refreshed and renewed.

The Rosary

This traditional prayer has been called "the great Catholic mantra." I can't remember who said that nor can I explain why, even though I think I understand. The rosary calls simultaneously for verbal prayer (silent or otherwise) and meditation on one of the Mysteries, that is, significant moments in the life of Jesus and Mary drawn from the Scripture. Even though I am no longer a member of the Catholic Church, I still say the rosary—only a decade at a time, usually. In times of stress, of confusion, of deep emotion, it is a calming, reflective way to pray.

The rosary has also been adopted by mainstream Protestants, who can use a lovely ecumenical version in which the Mysteries differ somewhat and the Jesus Prayer is used in place of the Hail Mary on the decades. There are several versions of the Jesus Prayer, but the most familiar is "Lord Jesus Christ, Son of the Living God, have mercy on me, a sinner." This is truly a beautiful prayer, speaking a truth from deep within. But when I do say the rosary, I say the traditional version. I simply cannot pray the Rosary without the Hail Mary. For most of us cradle Catholics, Mary is still our mother, as well as Mother of God.

Intercessory Prayer

Prayer is sometimes divided into four categories: adoration (or, a better word, *love*), thanksgiving, contrition, and petition. Some spiritual writers dismiss prayers of petition as "gimme prayers," but others see in them both depth and compassion. We pray not only for ourselves and our needs, but also for the needs of others. We pray this kind of prayer in the Lord's Prayer, asking for guidance, sustenance, forgiveness, and our "daily bread." We pray intercessory prayers in the privacy of our homes and during worship services. And we offer prayers of petition at candlelight vigils and funerals and celebrations of all kinds.

A more challenging question arises: What about *unanswered* prayer? Some people say prayers are *always* answered, just not necessarily in the way we want or expect. I don't find this to be a very satisfactory answer, especially for people in times of extreme trial, suffering, or stress. If you are starving, I don't think God answers your prayer for daily bread with a "no," even though bread all too often does not appear.

One response to this dilemma may be that the bread will not appear as an answer to prayer unless we help make it happen. We are called not just to pray for others, but also to help in the response—to serve as God's hands, feet, and heart. We are sometimes even called to serve as God's voice, although this probably happens rarely or less frequently than self-proclaimed prophets might think. And we are called to help care for the planet God gave us. If we don't help, God can't either.

I know this isn't a complete or satisfactory answer. I believe that a loving God wills our good, but I also know that it doesn't always happen—not at least here, in this life. I surely hope that it *will* happen—someday, somewhere, in some way.

I can think of two metaphors that speak to me about unanswered prayer. One is that of being a parent. We parents can and do hope for good for our children, for happiness, compassion, love. We can try to foster all of this, but we cannot guarantee it. When things are difficult for our children, our hearts and love are with them, but we may not be able bring things to a different, better, or right conclusion for them. They have to do their part as well. This doesn't explain those unanswered prayers, but I think most parents cannot help but understand.

I'll get to the second metaphor shortly. In the meantime, a quick look at prayer in the Scriptures.

The Scriptures speak of prayer in various times and in various situations. The book of Psalms is sort of all-occasion spiritual library, appealing to the best in us, the most vulnerable in us, and sometimes the far-from-the-best in us (for example, in the desire for vengeance). The psalmist cries out to God in joy, supplication, complaint, confidence, or…you name it.

In the New Testament, Jesus calls out to God in prayer several times. Here are a few examples. He prays after the cure of the leper: "As often as possible Jesus withdrew to out-of-the-way places for prayer" (Luke 5:16). He prays after the miracle of the loaves and fishes. That's when it begins to dawn on the disciples just who Jesus is. (See Luke 9:10-20.) He prays at Gethsemane, or the Mount of Olives, after the Last Supper, as he awaits his time of trial praying, "My Father, if there is any way, get me out of this. But please, not what I want. You, what do *you* want?" (Matthew 26:39). Is Jesus' prayer answered? He doesn't get out of this time of trial. In fact, he accepts the cross.

Throughout her life, his mother Mary probably experienced some unanswered prayers as well as witnessing the direction of her son's life and ministry, especially as his arrest, suffering, and death. But, as I explained earlier, death is not the end, and was not for Jesus.

When Jesus next speaks in the Gospels, it is not in prayer but in greeting and blessing the disciples, men and women both. The time of sorrow and terror have passed. Now it is one of astonishment and joy. And as for the disciples, that wonderful, clueless, insightful, ragtag, extraordinary, frightened, courageous, grieving, and joyous group? They have finally *begun* to get it. They will ultimately continue his mission, but first they immerse themselves in prayer. "And they were on their knees, worshiping him. They returned to Jerusalem bursting with joy. They spent all of their time in the Temple praising God. Yes" (Luke 24:52-53).

Now, that second metaphor.... It's not mine actually, but one I heard many, many years ago from a Capuchin priest during a Lenten service. In *The Master Weaver*, God weaves the pattern of our lives, a pattern that, when completed, will be a masterpiece of color, design, and meaning. Unfortunately for us, in this life we can only see the rough side of the masterpiece, that is, the side with the muddled colors, dangling threads, and indistinct pattern. Only at the end of the Master's work, that is, at the end of our lives on earth, will we see the finished pattern in all its beauty. Even if this is an imperfect metaphor, I—imperfect as I am—still like it. So I will still pray for myself and others as people have been doing for thousands of years.

This is my prayer for you and for me and for all who need it. It is from St. Paul's letter to the Ephesians.

I ask the Father to strengthen you by his Spirit—not a brute strength but a glorious inner strength—that Christ will live in you as you open the door and invite him in. And I ask him that with both feet planted firmly on love, you'll be able to take in with all followers of Jesus the extravagant dimensions of Christ's love. Reach out and experience the breadth! Test its length! Plumb the depths! Rise to the heights! Live full lives, full in the fullness of God (Ephesians 3:17-19).

25 PAST AND PRESENT
A LÁ REPRISTINATION
The Work of Restoration

God grant me the serenity to accept the things I cannot change;
the courage to change the things I can; and the wisdom to know
the difference.

— Reinhold Niebuhr

I like beginnings—New Year's Day, birthdays (usually), the beginning of
Advent, even Ash Wednesday and the beginning of Lent (although not
as much as the others). I also like days like December 21, 2012, which,
according to the Mayan calendar, ushered in a new 5,125-year epoch.
The world didn't end, of course. The Mayans never said it would. They
meant, instead, that it was the beginning of a new time.

So, with my penchant for new beginnings, it's natural that I like
the word *repristinate*.

No, I hadn't heard the word either until Pastor Monte Johnson
used it at a meeting at Immanuel, simultaneously introducing the word
and bringing all other business momentarily to a halt.

According to the dictionary, the first known use of the word was in
1659. It comes from the word *pristine*, meaning "pure." Along the way
someone added the prefix *re*, meaning to do it "again," and the suffix
ate, which makes it a verb. There you have it: *repristinate*. And of course,
modification didn't stop there. Now we have a noun: *repristination*.

One of the challenges of growing older is making *mistakes*—big,
small, and in-between ones. We elderly have had ample time and opportunity to make so many. We can't roll back time and undo or redo our

mistakes, even if we now know just what we should have done instead. Or, at least we *think* we do. We don't, of course, know all the mistakes we *might* have made if we had done things differently. Nevertheless, we can spend a lot of time and energy thinking that if we keep looking at the past we might make the present and the future turn out all right.

Some things we can change. Some things we can't. And it's important to know the difference. Who could have said it better—more clearly, simply, and succinctly—than Reinhold Niebuhr in his Serenity Prayer above? "God grant me...the wisdom to know the difference."

One thing we *can* begin to change is the way we look at things. We can recognize that life, change, hope, and all sorts of other things are part of an ongoing *process*. Using the image of life as a journey, we have to say we aren't *there* yet, wherever or whatever *there* is. And at this point, since no one has returned to tell about it, only God knows exactly what the ultimate *it* means. (Yes, Jesus returned from the dead, but he didn't talk about being dead. He talked about how to live.)

So what do we do, then, with all those yesterdays that keep on affecting our todays and tomorrows? Well, what we have is *today*. And when we think about it, that is quite enough. We can try to make the most of it or at least make a good start. We can repristinate.

I was going to say that, given all this mess and muddle that we sometimes drag forward, I find the idea of repristination quite glorious, but it is probably more mundane, like the legend of Lambin leftovers. Back when my husband was alive and my children were young and I was cooking for a family, I was the unelected Queen of Leftovers. There was a thoroughly unfounded rumor, initiated by my children, that one or another item reappeared on the daily menu in one form or another for years. That isn't true. A week, maybe, but that was the extent of it. But in repristinating, we are, in a sense, using leftovers to make something new and hopefully better. We discard some ingredients, we keep others, we add new elements, we decide how to cook it or not, and we add some original creative touches. And, voila! Past and Present a lá Repristination.

We all have regrets—things we wish we had done, things we wish we hadn't, and things we wish we'd done differently. That's part of being human, part of life, a potentially constructive part of learning and growing. Imperfect as we are, we have all at some point, at some time, done some harm to someone else, to our community, to ourselves. Small or significant, we have done it. If people say they have no regrets in life, they haven't been paying attention.

Here are some suggestions for a Repristination Starter Kit.

- We first have to recognize that some things need change and renewal and some don't. If we don't pay attention, how will we know what needs renewing? How will we even start?

- We can't *redo*, but we can *renew*. Repristination as used here does *not* mean making things just as they were before, restoring them exactly and precisely to their original condition. It means keeping what should be kept, discarding what should be discarded, and, yes, having the wisdom to know the difference.

- Repristination is a process. We don't have to complete it today, or tomorrow, or the day after. And, each time around, we don't have to do it perfectly and permanently.

- Repristination is an individual concern and also a matter for the community. We can draw help from family, friends, strangers, colleagues, one-time adversaries, and people we still find just a *wee bit* difficult. And we can give help to all those people too.

- Also, if we decide to be better listeners, to be more patient or more forthcoming, we are not doing it alone. We are listening, being patient, or forthcoming with *someone* or *something* else.

- In implementing (or ignoring) Plans A to E and beyond, it's a good idea to listen for the promptings of the Spirit.

- And finally, we always draw on, are sustained by, and are surrounded by God's grace.

I began this chapter with a quotation. I'm going to conclude with yet another. At a weekend retreat, the leader projected this quotation on the screen. It was later was echoed in a meeting. To me it is a beautiful expression of the deepest meaning of repristination.

This life, therefore, is not godliness but the process of becoming godly, not health but getting well, not being but becoming, not rest but exercise. We are not now what we shall be, but we are on the way. The process is not yet finished, but it is actively going on. This is not the goal but it is the right road. At present, everything does not gleam and sparkle, but everything is being cleansed.

These words sound contemporary, don't they? They sound as if they could have been penned—or keyboarded—yesterday or last year or last decade or maybe at least at the end of the last century—the *twentieth* century, that is. These words, however, were written nearly five hundred years ago in the early sixteenth century by a man named Martin Luther.

26 UNEXPECTED, REFLECTED
Surprised by Grace

What can I give back to God
for the blessings he's poured out on me?
— Psalm 116:12

The word *grace* covers a wide range of usages and concepts. We may say grace before meals as a blessing and grace after meals as thanksgiving. A hostess or host who makes everyone feel welcome is gracious. We may describe someone who moves smoothly with a kind of elegance as graceful. Someone who responds well and wisely to a difficult situation or conversation is said to have acted with grace. In England, a duke, duchess, and archbishop are formally addressed as "Your Grace." In music a grace note enhances or ornaments a regular note. And Elvis Presley's former home and current tourist attraction is, of course, Graceland.

So, how do I understand grace in terms of loss and transition?

a. A slow or sudden insight into something significant in my life and/or the community.

b. The strength to get out of a destructive situation or relationship.

c. The strength and courage to develop and sustain constructive relationships.

d. The wisdom to speak out appropriately and at the right time.

e. The ability to resist the impulse to speak out inappropriately or at the wrong time.

f. The generosity of spirit to care for and give to others.

g. The wisdom to do the caring well.

h. Knowing when and how to stand up for myself.

i. Knowing when and how to stand down.
j. Finding motivation and comfort in knowing that God loves me.
k. The comfort in knowing God loves me, as me, even if I don't know it yet.
l. Constructing the *new* normal.
m. None of the above.
n. All of the above and more.

The correct answer here is *n*, but please note the "more." What a wonderful and unexpected thing grace can be.

The definition of *grace* in *The American Heritage Collegiate Dictionary* has ten parts. One part refers to grace in a general theological or spiritual sense as "divine love and protection bestowed freely on people." In Christian usage it is "the state of being protected or sanctified by the favor of God." Note that nowhere does the dictionary define grace in terms of *limitation* or *exclusion*, but rather of in terms of *freely-given* love and protection. The dictionary is off to a good start, but there's even more I'd like to add.

First of all, as first part of the above definition points out, God's grace is free and freely given. It is not earned. It is not bought. It is like air—except that, fortunately, it isn't polluted and it isn't as thin as it is on mountaintops. It surrounds us. It's within us. It's just *there*. And *here*.

In addition, as Paul pointed nearly two thousand years ago, grace abounds. (See Romans 5:20-21.) It is an unlimited renewable resource. If you appear to have a lot of grace in the way you deal with others, it doesn't mean that I will have less. In fact, I can even draw from your example without taking anything away. And, fortunately, we can't use grace up. There isn't a bottom line here. God doesn't say "Sorry, you've currently used up your grace credit line. You will need to wait for further grace until the next billing period." (Good thing for me it works that way. I would probably be permanently overdrawn.) I can use all the grace God offers, even if I too often may not use it well.

Second, grace is universal. We are *all* God's children. God holds grace out to *all of us* with both hands, so to speak. "Here it is, my beloved. Come and get it. Come one. Come all."

In this respect, I become very uncomfortable when I hear someone speaking in a religious context of "the others," that is, people who believe otherwise than us or are not believers they way we are. It seems as if their gifts, generosity of spirit, and essential kindness don't matter. They are beyond the pale. When we make judgments about the worthiness of others, we pretty much make God's vision as limited as our own.

It makes me even more uncomfortable to see a certain unholy relish expressed by those who have this limited vision. It is as if they see no point in being invited into heaven unless others are shut out, permanently and quite unpleasantly. It is a sort of spiritual *schadenfreude*. That's a handy German expression for taking joy in the misfortunes of others. "Just wait. *They'll* see…. And, thank goodness, they ain't me."

We can, of course, turn this thinking around, believing that a lot of people are going to be pleasantly surprised and happy to find themselves in a heaven they didn't believe in during their earthly sojourn. Personally, I would be pleasantly surprised and happy and relieved to find myself in one I *do* believe in!

Yes, grace it is a gift to be accepted thankfully, used well, shared generously, and not hoarded. Grace helps us to do small acts of kindness, even bigger ones, any size we can imagine. Grace helps us accept kindness—how else?—*gracefully*. The word *grace* appears throughout in the New Testament. Look up some of the references in a concordance or bible dictionary and see how it flows through God's word so graciously, like a river watering and bringing life to the land.

And, finally, grace can come, or be recognized, at the most unexpected moments, including when we need it most. It can also come in the small, seemingly ordinary moments when we suddenly, or gradually, become aware of God's presence. It can come in the sound of rain that ends a drought, in the voice of someone we love, in a hug of a child, or in the nearness of an animal companion. It can come in a shared meal or a quiet cup of tea. It can come in the beauty of a sunrise or a sunset. Wait a moment. For those of us who don't like getting up really early, mid-morning is a possibility too. I could go on and on, but I won't. Make your own list if you'd like, and be sure to highlight the times when you are surprised by grace. You'll be surprised.

Many decades ago, a retreat leader in Iowa began each session with these words: "Let us place ourselves in the presence of God." At a Saturday morning Centering Prayer session a few months ago, I was trying to do just that. It isn't generally easy for me because it's so easy to find myself in the presence of Me and My Distractions. But, in this case, for a brief moment, I *did* have a sense of Divine Presence. The word *awesome* is over-used, but I can't think of another word to describe the sense of the Presence beyond Time, beyond the Galaxies, almost like distant streaks of light in vast unknown darkness. *Someone was there.* And then, suddenly my perspective shifted. Yes, God was out *there* but also *here*, not distant, not beyond, but *here*, close, right beside me, all around me—like the oxygen we breathe.

The experience didn't last long, perhaps only minutes. It was soon followed, of course, by the Distraction Team. In the interim, I felt an immense sense of gratitude for the insight, if you want to call it that, but I also recognized that this sudden, surprising, and gratuitous gift of grace certainly wasn't merited. Still more, it certainly wasn't meant just for me. It was meant to be *shared*. So I am adding it here, to this section, for anyone who wishes to share that moment of grace.

The Apostle Paul uses the word *grace* a lot in his greetings to other disciples and friends, in both the beginning and ending of his letters. I've used a lot of quotations in these chapters, but in this case, I can't think of any better borrowed ending than this one.

"The amazing grace of the Master, Jesus Christ, the extravagant love of God, the intimate friendship of the Holy Spirit, be with all of you" (2 Corinthians 13:14).

EPILOGUE
Helen's Brick-and-Mortar Maxims

The maxims in the following collection are not in any particular order of significance, assuming they have significance. They are arranged more less in the order they came to me over my eighty-one-and-still-counting years.

1. We don't have to like some experiences, and it is not abnormal not to like them. "I hate being a widow! I hate being a widow!" I raged in that first year to Father Carl Dehne, the Jesuit priest noted in the dedication of this book. "That's probably a good thing," he said mildly. "It might be really strange if you liked it." He was right. It would have been. You live—and grow—through these experiences, but nobody said they'd be fun.

2. Change is not termination. Long ago, when I was in high school— never mind how long ago—our high school physics text noted the following: "Matter and energy can neither be created nor destroyed." The out-dated text had been published before the confirmation of atomic energy, in which matter is dramatically, with far-reaching consequences, changed into energy. To bring the books up to date, someone had carefully added in ink in each book: "It can only be changed in form." My daughter Jeanne reminded me of this standard law of physics when my husband, Henry, died. I do not believe his beautiful energy and spirit was extinguished—it was changed in form.

3. Not 24/7—Please call again. I do not believe our loved ones who have passed on are necessarily available every minute of the eternal day.

Wouldn't that cast a shadow on eternal bliss? Those we love very likely did not listen to every single word we said *during* our life together. Why should they have to do so *after* death? Quiet intervals are perfectly normal and necessary. What I *do* believe is that death does not kill love. Their love for us remains, and so does ours for them.

4. Alternative mistakes. "If I had it to do over again, there are certainly things I would do differently." Many of us have said this at one time or another—or maybe many times. And we very likely would. But on the other hand, as wise observers have noted, we might make a whole different set of mistakes. (How true—at least for me. See below.)

5. Learning by experience—or not. One of my favorite quotations is: "Good judgment comes from experience, and experience comes from bad judgment." The quote has been variously attributed to sources including the homespun philosopher Will Rogers but, according to Dr. James Jay Horning, the original source was the great sufi thinker, Mulla Nasrudin. We all know what it means to do things the hard way. It's nice to know that mistakes can sometimes be recycled, sort of like composting fallen and spoiled fruit for garden growth.

6. Conversation is not a spectator sport. It is a full-participation one. Support groups have rules in place so that everyone gets a fair share of "air time." In an informal group, conversation is a back-and-forth and around-and-around sort of thing. If some group members consistently dominate, it is usually not because they are so interesting but because everyone else is so polite. Native American and Buddhist wisdom tells us that God gave us two ears and one mouth so that we would listen more than we talk.

7. Patience required. It can sometimes be really difficult to be patient with other people, but it can be even more difficult to be the one requiring patience from other people.

8. Skills still. My mother once said: "One of the hardest things about growing old is that you can no longer help other people." "Well, you help me," I told her, "just by being there for me." Even if you can no longer do some of the things you once could or now do them quite differently, people may be really glad you're still around, just because you are you.

9. Pay it multidirectionally or whatever. Pay it forward, pay it backward, pay it sidewise, up, down, or out, but when you can, give something back. Other people have done it for me. And for you.

10. Keep doing as long as you can. My husband, Henry, said, "As you grow older, be careful about the things you stop doing, because you may not start doing them again."

11. Right, wrong, and ? It's bad to feel you are always wrong. It's hard on you, and it can be hard on everyone around you. It can be even harder to feel you are always right. That is certainly hard on everyone around you, and in the long run, it usually won't work out that well for you either.

12. Infallibility. Speaking of always being right, I think there is such a thing as Infallibility, but it is limited to Three Persons—the Trinity. They don't go around talking about it much. They have better things to do, care about, and worry about.

13. Incarnation cosmology. Small things can comfort, small things can harm, small things can confuse, and small things can lead to amazing big things. Look around you and far beyond. Remember it all started with an infinitesimally small Big Bang. God can do a lot with small things.

14. Incarnation and creation. If the Incarnation has been part of your life long enough, it is easy to take it for granted. But think about it. God came down and walked around among us and ate and drank with us—by choice. I picture the Trinity talking together one eternal morning about 2,000-plus years ago. And Father/Mother God says something like, "Things are not going all that well on Planet Earth. They just don't seem to get what it means to live as our beloved children. One of us should go there and do something about it. Give a living example of what it means." So One of the Three says, "I'll go." And One did.

15. Changing some outcomes in the midst of uncertainties. We may think the Golden Rule is first mentioned in the New Testament. After all, that's where it's expressed so beautifully in word and in the witness of Jesus' life. But the idea was around for centuries before Jesus walked the earth. Bad things can and do, alas, happen to good people, but it is pretty hard to argue with the idea of treating others as you wish they would treat you.

16. Faith is not a club for "members only." Faith is a gift, a response, a process, an experience that far exceeds what we can define, control, or comprehend. Nobel laureate physicist Richard Feynman said, "If you think you understand quantum mechanics, you don't understand quantum mechanics." I say, "If you think you have the fullness of faith, you don't."

17. Called and calling you. Being loved by God is a call. We all receive this call, but we respond in different ways. We are called and invited to share God's love with others just as we, in turn, hope to receive it. Sometimes our responses can differ because of circumstances, especially since, in many areas, there isn't a level playing field, at least not in human terms. People face terribly challenging circumstances—isolation, difficult family circumstances, you name it. God needs our help in leveling that playing field with our hard "work"—using our "shovels" and adding "soil." What does that mean for you?

18. Unintended imitation. "Always let the *other* person be the idiot." So says my daughter Rosemary. In other words, try to avoid doing or becoming the very thing you deplore in others.

19. Interesting/interested/interim. Keep up old interests and/or develop new ones. So what if you are going to be fifty or sixty or seventy or...? You don't have quite so many years left to develop or pursue your interests. Do you really want to spend that time being bored?

20. Growing old gracefully or in style. We may not share other people's ideas of how to grow old gracefully. As long as it is constructive and not destructive to yourself or to other people, your own style is your own. One size does not fit all. Keep reading.

21. Early eccentricity. There is something to be said for being rather eccentric while you are still considered more or less young. That way, when you're older and eccentric, people will at least know you're consistent and won't be able go around using that patronizing phrase, "senior moment."

22. Changeless change. Change happens with or without our consent—good change, unpleasant change, and who-the-hell-knows-what-at-this-time change. So I'll go for the beautiful Serenity Prayer, "God grant me the courage to change the things I can change; the courage to accept the things I cannot change; and the wisdom to know the difference."

23. Regrets. One of the more painful parts of transitions is recognizing too late—five minutes later, twenty-five years later—what you *should* or *should not* have done, what you *should* or *should not* have said. Ouch! It is generally preferable not to hold on to regrets, but we do need to acknowledge mistakes, learn from them, and move on. Regrets are a common and often necessary part of growth for both individuals and communities.

24. Helping the prophets. There are times to speak out and times *not* to speak out. It takes practice and perspective to learn the difference.

25. Learning forgiveness. Practicing forgiveness is vital to life and sanity. Practicing vengeance leads to an endless cycle of violence and pain. It can be easier to forgive when you or those you love are not the ones hurting. In fostering forgiveness in others, try to understand the depth of their hurt. Oh, yes. In addition to learning to forgive others, we may learn that *we're* the ones who need to seek forgiveness.

26. Friend focus. It can help your perspective to ask yourself if you'd like to be *your own* friend.

27. Little things. There can be a lot of satisfaction in "little" things—a cup of tea, a friend's phone call, a warm blanket, a good book, a purring cat, an attentive dog, a spring rain, the beauty of (not too much) snow, and so on, and so on. We need to enjoy the little things which are, after all, in greater supply than the big things.

28. Prayer: past and present imperfect. Take time to pray *today* even if you haven't done so for a while or for a long while. God's love doesn't have an expiration date. Don't worry about doing it *well*. It's about communication and relationship, not winning a contest. *Everyone wins when we pray.*

29. Being and becoming yourself. Remember to work on being your renewed, improved self, not someone else's idea of who you should be. As the saying goes, no one can be yourself better than you.

30. "God's holy light surrounds us." This is the beginning of the meditation ritual I've incorporated in a lot of settings after learning it from Sister Fran Glowinksi. As you light a candle, say, "God's holy light surrounds us. Only good can come in. Only good can go out." I also use these words at the end of rituals. It's a fitting prayer to bring this book to a close. "As we extinguish the candle, we take the light with us. For ourselves and to share with others."

ACKNOWLEDGMENTS

At my age I have a lot to acknowledge: people, pets, places, blessings, regrets, and surprises. But space is limited here, so I'll stick to people.

So, first of all, I'd like to thank the gifted Patricia Lynch, editor of this book, for her insights, dedicated work, and expertise! My thanks also to daughter Rosemary who does the first reading and comments well and wisely on everything I write before it leaves the house. And as always, my thanks to Gregory Augustine Pierce, spirited voice for faith, books, and social justice.

I am surely grateful for my children Joe, Rosemary, and Jeannefor their love and understanding and for who they are. And my thanks and blessings also to their spouses/significant others—Suzette, Scott, and Skip—and my special granddaughter, Jessica. My heart will always hold my beloved husband, Henry J. Lambin, R.I.P. His wisdom, humor, and kindness remain with me still. And so too does my heart hold my loving parents, Verto and Helen Reichert.

Then there are my dear sister, Vera; my late sister-in-law, Margaret; and the sisters in spirit who have lovingly put up with me along the way, among them: Nancy, Dorothy (two), Ann, Jean (two) Michele, Jennifer, Maria, Sis, Mickey, Phyllis (two), Darlene, Lea, Louise, Susan, Cathy, Janice, Anne, Dale, Kari, Theresa, Marge, and other special people— including Mike and other brothers in spirit—each a gift much appreciated and not necessarily deserved.

I would also like to thank the readers of this book, because to me you are friends known and unknown.

And finally I would like to thank the Very Reverend John David Van Dooren, Rector; my sponsors/friends Howell Browne and Phyllis Robb; and the people of Church of the Atonement for the grace and warmth of their welcome to this pilgrim's new spiritual home.

ABOUT THE AUTHOR

Helen Reichert Lambin was born in 1933 (the year the Volstead Act was repealed) and grew up in Iowa, which will always be a part of her. She has lived in the Second City for decades. It was here that she met her beloved husband, Henry Lambin, now deceased, the inspiration for the book, *Death of a Husband.* She has been wife, mother, grandmother, mother-in-law, and grandmother willingly. She has also been student, pet companion, and writer (willingly), worker (willingly and otherwise), and widow (very unwillingly).

Helen has worked as a secretary, copywriter, caseworker, event planner, and occasional film extra. Her writing has centered on finding meaning and hope during times of difficulty, loss, and change. She has been profiled in print, on television (including *The Today Show*), and on the internet as one of the more senior women who have acquired serious tattoo art. She is the author of *From Grief to Grace* and *Prayers for Sleepless Nights*, as well as chapters in *An Irrepressible Hope* and short articles on baseball and travel. She is now working on a book on mourning the deaths of adults siblings or best friends.

Also by Helen Lambin

THE DEATH OF A HUSBAND

PRAYERS FOR SLEEPLESS NIGHTS

and selections in

AN IRREPRESSIBLE HOPE:
NOTES FROM CHICAGO CATHOLICS

HIDDEN PRESENCE: TWELVE BLESSINGS
THAT TRANSFORMED SORROW OR LOSS

DIAMOND PRESENCE: TWELVE STORIES
OF FINDING GOD AT THE OLD BALL PARK

Additional Grief Resources

CATHOLIC AND MOURNING A LOSS
Sr. Mauryeen O'Brien

THE NEW DAY JOURNAL:
A JOURNAL FROM GRIEF TO HEALING
Sr. Mauryeen O'Brien

GRIEVING WITH MARY
Mary K. Doyle

Available from booksellers or call
800-397-2282 / actapublications.com